THE
SINGLE BEST
INVESTMENT

THE
SINGLE BEST
INVESTMENT

2nd Edition

CREATING WEALTH
with DIVIDEND GROWTH

LOWELL MILLER

Distributed to the book trade by: Independent Publishers Group, 814 North Franklin Street, Chicago, IL 60610, (312) 337–0747.

This publication is designed to provide accurate and authoritative information with regard to the subject matter covered. It is sold with the understanding that the publisher is not engaged in rendering legal, accounting, or other professional advice. If legal advice or other expert assistance is required, the services of a competent professional should be sought.

— From a *Declaration of Principles* jointly adopted by a Committee of the American Bar Association and a Committee of Publishers and Associations

SECOND EDITION

ISBN-13: 978-0-9651750-8-1
ISBN-10: 0-9651750-8-1

ACKNOWLEDGMENTS

For all my friends and colleagues at Miller/Howard and Overlook: you're always the best . . .

TABLE OF CONTENTS

INTRODUCTION

A Typical Situation

Not long ago a friend came into my office, looking kind of glum and depressed. I couldn't imagine why he'd be feeling so down; after all, he's the founder and sole owner of a fantastic business which dominates its field nationally and grows by more than 40% per year. He was making a mint, and had a lovely new wife. The two of them were almost finished moving into a perfect estate, and were happy as lovebirds. The picture was mostly flawless, but K. was bothered about his savings and investment.

"I simply feel lost with it," he said, a most remarkable and unusual look of defeat in his eyes, "I don't feel like I can count on the advice I get, and it seems like every time I buy a fund it comes in running last. Then I watch some guy on TV and I'm off in a different direction all over again. I think I must be too busy with my work to really get this right."

He took out a fistful of brokerage and mutual fund company statements to show me his array of holdings. I was reminded of Miller's Law of Investment, which goes something like this: if you give people the opportunity to invest their money by merely making a phone call, they will.

There was no rhyme or reason or philosophy in his holdings; each item had its own justification. A newspaper article. A money manager on Wall Street Week. The maker of a hot product selling well in the local grocery store. A newsletter tip. Cocktail guidance from a friend whose cousin's father's uncle is in the financial business in the next town over from Silicon Valley.

What did he imagine? That because he was good in a business of making and selling things that he would also be a good (or lucky) securities analyst and investor? Would he next try to pull his own teeth, or write his own brief in court?

I don't think K. is unique, except perhaps in his ability to recognize, finally, his own limitations. As investment possibilities have proliferated—there are 9,000 mutual funds today compared with less than 1,000 in 1975, and over 20,000 investable domestic stocks compared with 6,000 just 20 years ago—so have the media which hope to attract the advertising dollars that push those new products.

Where investment was in the past the province of the rich and an afterthought for the middle class, now it is everyone's hobby. Business fandom is as large as the crowd for sports results, the weather, or news of the latest presidential scandal. Now, on break, factory workers talk more about their 401(k)s than about the opening of fishing season.

Information Everywhere

And the Information Age has made it possible for investors to quickly and easily learn about their investments, follow the short-term price movements of their investments, research new investments. There is so much information floating about in the airwaves that it seems to permeate one's dental fillings.

In recent years the press, radio, TV, the internet, brokers, and mutual fund companies have simply flooded the public with information about business and investing. There are experts behind every tree today, pros lurking in doorways, wise men selling shares and annuities.

Every day you're told about some great new idea that a mutual fund manager is buying, some undiscovered concept this brokerage firm thinks will outshine the moon. Magazines regularly list the hottest mutual funds and stockpickers, tormenting you if you're not "in" these things, tempting you to jump on board. Every day, the Dow is up so much, the Dow is down so much, you get daily small pleasures, daily small pains. It's another new record high, it's a new record high, a new record high! What a great country!

You've got your young guys running racy small-cap growth funds, your middle-aged managers running seasoned large-cap growth, your fuddy-duddies in old-fashioned clothes advocating the value of "value," your number-crunching consultant and financial planners extolling the holy salvation of asset allocation. Someone does a study that says you'll do well buying last year's winners. Someone else does a study clearly proving that if you buy last year's winners you'll end up in the poorhouse. A man with a bow tie asserts the coming threat of inflation . . . and keeps sounding his alarm for years and years. Alan Greenspan warns of "irrational exuberance" but you don't know what to make of that since everything else he says is totally indecipherable.

And in your junk mail: *Sell Everything Now. The Mother of All Crashes May Have Already Begun. Just $20 for a Three-Month Trial!*

The barrage of information aimed at investors like so many stinger missiles jangles the nerves, and produces more confusion than illumination. The proliferation of possibilities may be fantastic, but at the same time it's disheartening. How can an investor—someone who's typically not a professional but who has important funds that must be properly invested—possibly keep up with the flow of news, the flow of ideas, the flow of advice that so often contradicts even the most recent piece of advice that had flowed past only days or hours ago? It's enough to make you want to bury yourself up to your neck in T-bills! This is pretty much the state my friend K. was in when he came to see me.

"Everything that was good for the market yesterday is no good for it today."

Whom to believe? *What* to believe? *Where's* the best place to put your money? Does the answer vary with each investor's situation? By a lot? By a little? Do you have to change where you put your money all the time, depending on conditions in the market? Do you have to be able to guess where interest rates are going in order to succeed in the markets?

Should you be in Growth Stocks? Value Stocks? Small Stocks? Mid-Caps? International? Emerging Markets? IPO's? Vulture Funds? REITs? High Tech? Low Tech? No Tech? Bonds? Mutual Funds? Managed Accounts? The question comes up again and again: *What to do? What to do?*

Is There a Simple Strategy that Makes Sense and Works?

There *should* be some way to have a <u>simple</u> investment program that <u>makes sense</u>, that's <u>easy</u> to implement, and that has a <u>high chance of succeeding</u> in meeting your long-term investment goals at the end of the road.

There is—if you're a long-term investor; and that's what this book is about—a single simple approach that can serve as the primary investment vehicle for nearly every reader. If you want to try to guess the hot sector for next year, or which of the 9,000 mutual funds will outperform this quarter, or which tech company will win the networking wars—you've picked up the wrong guide. There's nothing in it for you. This book is for savers and builders, for people who understand (or who want to understand) that the forces of time, modest and reliable growth, and compounding are on their side. Investing isn't some athletic event where agility and flashes of virtuosity are the secrets of success. Rather, investing really *is* investing—the methodical accumulation of capital through a sensible and disciplined plan which recognizes that "shares" are not little numbers that jump around in the paper every day. They represent *a partnership interest in a real and going business.* Your plan, very simply, must recognize that you will manage your investments by actually being an investor—a passive partner in a real and going business.

The Goal of This Book

In this book I'll detail a simple and straightforward way to earn solid returns on your investments over the long term, with the lowest possible risk. It's an approach that can get you off the hook of information addiction, free you from the need to constantly keep up with the latest developments and the opinions of a million pundits. In effect, you can invest in stocks without "playing the market."

This strategy is not a trick, it doesn't require that you learn a new language or play around with options or futures or anything exotic. You can do it yourself—though many investors may decide to work with a broker or investment manager.

One goal, in addition to seeing your capital grow, is to sleep well at night. Who wants high returns at the cost of a lifetime of worry and anxiety? Perhaps a few compulsive people would make that trade, but I think most of us would prefer to enjoy this brief sojourn on the blue planet with as little angst as possible. One of the ideas behind this approach is that the "slings and arrows of outrageous fortune" will bounce off your toughened skin, because you'll understand the foundation of your investment, and you'll understand, I hope, that it is a *true investment,* not some speculative game cooked up by business school grads on Wall Street.

To be sure, your portfolio will go up and down—this can never be avoided if you hope to have reasonably good long-term gains—but the downs won't bother you because you'll understand exactly why prices have declined, you'll know when prices are due to rebound, and you'll have extremely high confidence and a clear vision that prices will rise over the long term. You'll have this high confidence, as well as a high comfort level—two requirements for long-term success—because the strategy is based on impeccable *common sense.*

Common Sense, Comfort Level, and Investor Behavior

No investor can hope to succeed without having the ability to stick to a plan. This is decisively true in the often surprising and dramatic world of investing. You can't let your convictions be shaken, or you'll jump from pillar to post the moment times become difficult, and, in the end, have little to show for it. Yet only if you're *comfortable* with what you're doing will you be able to stick to your plan. And comfort (peace within and a cool head) in the frequently volatile world of investments is only achieved, I believe, when you are able to stand on the calm bedrock of common sense.

Common Sense

Common sense in investing means employing a strategy that's inextricably linked to the actual corporations in which you've invested. Investing is about being a *partial owner of a real business;* this fact should never be forgotten, and I'm sure I'll repeat it until you're totally annoyed.

Common sense means your strategy needs to be effective in virtually all market conditions (it may shine in some types of markets and be just okay in others, but it should never contain the seeds of even short-term catastrophe, if you're to maintain a calm mind as a strong holder).

Common sense means having reasonable, achievable goals. Common sense means never trying to hit a home run, and never berating yourself with remorse for a situation that doesn't work out. Common sense means spreading out your risks, but not so much that you lose control over your portfolio.

Comfort Level

The instant you deviate from a common sense approach, falling under the sway of a newsletter guru or a slick TV expert, or playing some "system" that's had a good record for a few years, you'll lose your comfort level because you're no longer grounded in the reality of being a part-owner of a real business.

And <u>when you lose your comfort level</u> you become fearful, greedy, superstitious, "intuitive," prayerful, victimized—you enter into all the emotional states that ultimately provoke investing mistakes.

In the first edition of this book we noted a Morningstar study showing that five-year returns for the average growth fund during the period ending December 31, 1995, were 12%. But average *investor* returns were only 2.5%. Why the difference? The fund may have been fine, but most investors, apparently, were buying at the tops and selling at the lows. Assets flowed into the funds after they'd had great years—prompting "the crowd" to jump aboard the shiny train—and flowed right back out when the previous pace could not be sustained. Ironically, "average" investors were most comfortable investing when the funds were highest, and least comfortable investing when the funds were cheapest. A recent study by Dalbar Associates confirms the eternal nature of this phenomenon. For the twenty years through 2004 (ten years later than the Morningstar study) the average fund investor earned 3.5%, compared with a market gain of 13%. The facts remain the same—even the spread difference between potential and actual remains the same—though the time periods measured were quite different.

One element present here—an element whose appearance in your own brain you should watch out for—is the natural tendency of the mind to *extrapolate* from the present. Remember when oil prices were rising in the late seventies? The experts extrapolated the rate of change and decided that by 1990 oil would sell for $100 a barrel. Well, by 1998 it declined to $16 per barrel. Ooops. In 1990 journalists were trying to paint a picture of the world's population totally decimated by AIDS within the decade. Many trends in society seem as if they're going to last forever, and the mind begins to extrapolate from here to there: but it's so busy extrapolating it forgets to think of all the things that could change the course of events. The failures that become successes, the successes that become failures. I keep an

8-track tape player in my basement to remind me that things don't always go as anticipated.

Investors are plagued by doubts and uncertainties, even when things are going well *(Should I sell now or wait for even more gains?)*. This is only natural, for the future is always ineffable, and in the unfolding future the market marks itself by price changes. Unlike other aspects of life, price changes can't be explained away, or rationalized, or denied. They just *are*. Prices, and therefore the market, are immutable and beyond our control. I'll be frank: I've never been able to wish a stock to a higher price. Prices make us feel powerless; it's no wonder that emotional comfort as an investor is hard to achieve.

Investor Behavior

In the relatively new field of Behavioral Finance, students of investor behavior have come to some startling conclusions, conclusions that shed all too much light on the mistakes most of us make and the weaknesses most of us have. These scholars and experimenters have quantified what successful investors have known since time began: it's not the vehicle that crashes, it's the nut behind the wheel.

After years and years of assuming that the economy and the markets are made up of rational actors making fully informed decisions, economists and finance researchers have finally come to understand that investors are actually human beings filled with hopes and dreams and fear and confusion. In other words, investors exhibit all the human frailties found in every other realm of living. Traits of character don't magically dissolve away the moment a person begins to act as an investor. A number of traits common to most investors—like extrapolation—have been identified, and we'll take a moment to look at a few of interest. Bear in mind that these are not *other people's* characteristics, they are yours and mine. They are *common* characteristics, and more than likely they're affecting you importantly:

1. *Duration is as important as magnitude.* Years ago Harvard psychology researchers showed that subjects could endure great levels of pain if they knew the pain would be gone in a short time. But if the subjects were made aware that the pain would last a long time, they suffered more and "gave up" much more quickly even if the actual pain level inflicted was quite modest. The financial world saw this phenomenon after the 1987 crash, when investors did cash in their fund shares, though at a much lower level than expected. It all happened so fast, there was really little time to feel anything, much less act. Afterwards, many investors became involved in waiting for their stocks to return to former prices, to get out even. Moderate levels of fund selling continued right on through the rising market of 1988. According to a recent Louis Harris poll, 78% of investors would sell their funds if the market declined 25% or more. The 1987 crash would have met that criteria, but investors didn't have a chance to feel the pain. Interestingly, that same survey showed that only 20% of investors would consider buying if stocks fell by 25% or more. Does this sound like a population that wants to buy low and sell high?

Investors intent on improving their results will want to keep these facts in mind, and try to behave contrary to the crowd, hard as that may often be. After all, the crowd is only responding to normal human emotions. Remember, duration is crucial. The longer a downtrend persists, the more difficult it will be to buy the lows, but that difficulty is only your susceptibility the principles of Behavioral Finance. As a downtrend drags on, whether in an individual stock or in the overall market, participants slowly throw in the towel, one by one, as they reach their individual pain thresholds. Eventually almost everyone is bearish—and almost everyone has already sold. It is from this fertile soil that most great rallies begin.

2. *Investors don't want to experience losses.* One reason investors are always waiting to get out even, is that they don't like to experience losses, which are a form of pain. In a number of studies, economist Richard Thaler of the University of Chicago found that losing $1 makes investors feel two to two-and-a-half times as bad as winning \$1 makes them feel good. A loss appears larger to most people than a gain of equal size. The reason investors wait to "get even" is that as long as they haven't sold, the loss is merely on paper; it can be, in effect, denied.

But when the loss is actually taken, a discrete event has occurred which cannot be pushed away from the investor's consciousness. The loss itself makes the investor feel quite literally like a loser, whereas in holding to "get even" the investor can travel a kind of self-deluded heroic route. Amos Tversky of Stanford University commented that "Loss aversion — the greater impact of the downside than the upside — is a fundamental principle of the human pleasure machine." This is easy to see in real life. Which gives you a stronger emotion: coming home with a new car, or having it smashed up by a drunk driver the next day?

In the realm of investing, the lesson is that most people have difficulty taking losses, and are more risk-averse than they realize or know. This is important for each of us to recognize. The highest probability is that you and I and anyone we know are in truth risk-averse, no matter what you or I or anyone we know may say. We need to be aware of it, because it has a direct impact on our investment decisions, most of which pretend to be rational but are actually heavily influenced by our character structures. As Frank Campanale, former CEO of Smith Barney Consulting Group, put it, "The fears of the client drive the investment process more than the knowledge of the financial adviser."

For example, loss aversion, according to Meir Statman, professor of finance at Santa Clara University, prompts investors to sell winning stocks too early. The pain of regret is more powerful than greed, he says. Investors with winning positions sell early in order to avoid the imagined regret they *will* have if they fail to realize the profits that they currently have. This is no academic theory. I've sold too early for emotional reasons many times, and I don't know anyone who hasn't.

3. *People compartmentalize their money issues.* Imagine that upon arriving at a Broadway theater you discover you've lost your $50 ticket. Would you pay another $50 for another ticket? Now let's say you arrive at the theater ready to buy a ticket and discover you've lost $50 in cash. It should be clear that in both cases you're out $50. But of subjects questioned only 46% said they'd buy another ticket if they'd lost the first one, while 88% said they'd still buy a ticket if they had just lost the cash. To buy a second ticket "doubles" the cost of the play in the mind of the buyer, while lost cash is in a more abstract compartment of the mind, and hasn't yet been "invested" in the play.

Likewise, as Richard Thaler has pointed out, most "normal" investors compartmentalize their money in seemingly irrational ways. People tend to be more aggressive with their money when the markets are ebullient—and that's why the markets become ebullient!—but become cautious when the market sours. Isn't this just the opposite of buying low and selling high? That's another reason why investors may hold on to a stock whose prospects have seriously dimmed, waiting to "get out even." That stock is put into a separate compartment, and stays there even if holding it directly contradicts all of the investor's stated principles and guidelines. Daniel Kahneman, of Princeton University, suggests that in the compartmentalizing process, "Investors focus on the risk of individual securities. As a result, they tend to fret over the short-term performance of each investment, often leading to excessive trading and bad decisions." A calm mind will generate better profits than a hot tip, you might say.

4. *Investors lack self-control.* In an unusual display of common sense for an economist, Thaler points out that in life we eat too much, we have a terrible time kicking old habits, we don't exercise enough, in general we aren't able to take control of ourselves as much as we'd like. Why should it be any different when it comes to investing? Why shouldn't we jump in with both eyes closed just as the market is hitting new highs and we can't stand holding so much cash anymore? Why shouldn't we bail out of a well-run mutual fund when it has underperformed the pack, even though we know its style has been out of favor and if we could just hold a bit longer or even buy more it might become a leader again? It's in our natures to try to be rational, but, in the end, we have a craving to believe others who've got a hypnotic or convincing story to tell, or to find impulsive release when we can no longer tolerate either the pain or the pleasure of our positions.

5. *Narcissism plays a role.* Thaler notes that investors, risk-averse as they may be, are also in some sense <u>over-confident</u>. Even amateur investors somehow believe their opinions are worth more than a cup of coffee, and most investors will continue to buy mutual funds, though most funds underperform, because they persist in believing they can pick winners. No matter what the facts say, investors will "buy" this theory or that, or this star fund manager or that, believing that they are somehow gifted with the ability to make distinctions in a world that is not only volatile, complex, and unpredictable, but is structured to extract fees from investors every time they make a decision. Investors are arrogant and rarely show the humility and respect that the markets deserve. Rather, they're like the bumpkin who sees a Picasso for the first time and exclaims, "My child could do better than that!" Maybe, maybe . . .

Open Your Inner Eyes

We could go on and on looking at the conundrums and complications of the hearts and minds of investors, but the brief discussion above should at least alert you to the fact that you're probably not making the sorts of rational decisions that you may have imagined yourself to be making, or might be capable of making. Much noise from the underworld intervenes. Emotions influence investment decisions like the moon directs the tides, and to succeed over the long term you've got to do more than open a brokerage account and keep your records. You've got to tune in to who you are, what you want, how you behave in various conditions, the kinds of change you might be capable of and the kinds you are not.

Awareness and control of the inner life is extremely important to successful investment. This is not just rhetoric or something that applies to "other" investors. It applies to all of us, and it's what makes markets volatile in the first place. To tell the truth, investors are flying off the handle everywhere you look.

When anxiety becomes intolerable we tend to believe that we can *do something* to alleviate the feelings of fear, of loss, of lack of control. More often than not, and nearly always when an investment strategy has been carefully considered in the first place, doing nothing would be the best decision any investor can make. But few are capable of riding comfortably with the waves. Most try to make a break for it and swim, but the shore is far, far away . . . always farther than it appears. Instead of returns on capital, many investors experience only frustration and bitterness.

Yet investing can be solid and comfortable, like a well-made old wool blanket, if you approach it sensibly. Part and parcel of a sensible approach, a commonsense approach, is to understand just who you are and the kinds of emotional reactions to investing that you experience—as well as how those reactions influence your decisions.

Investors need to learn not only the "rules" for identifying a potentially successful investment, but also to ask "How will I feel when buying it? How will I feel when holding it? How will I feel when selling a loser? How will I feel when selling a winner?" No one can exist in this life without emotions and their power as decision makers, so you might as well get to know them.

Most of us believe we can be good investors if only we can learn what "works." In part that's true. The strategy you use must be a sound one. But no strategy exists in a vacuum, it is always implemented, for better or worse, by a human being.

Any strategy must take account of the inherent emotionalism of the human mind and heart, and, after that accounting, emerge with a process that inspires faith and confidence in the long-term result.

Investors, Listen Up

You will <u>not</u> succeed if you trade a lot. You can only win the investment game by actually *being* an investor. This is true for amateurs, and the record of mutual funds proves it is true for most professionals as well. You will <u>not</u> succeed if you pick ten different stocks for ten different reasons, or ten different stocks because ten different "advisors" or brokers say they are good ones. You will <u>not</u> be successful if you constantly dream of larger profits than the market can reasonably be expected to provide.

You'll only succeed by gluing your eyes firmly to the long-term future, and by making *long-term commitments* within the structure of a strategy that's founded on reason and common sense, supported by historical evidence that the strategy has performed well in the past.

I think you'll find that the investment technique outlined in this book cuts through all the b.s. constantly being shoveled on investors by the press and by financial firms advertising their wares. It's both a systematic approach and a way of thinking and feeling which will stand you in good stead for the rest of your life. Hopefully, it will provide a kind of therapy for the kinds of investment foolishness—whether too conservative or too aggressive—that most of us experience. It doesn't always fit into the neat categories that you read about every day or hear about on television, but it is at the heart of a true understanding of investment. Getting to know this investment strategy is going to teach you nearly everything you need to know about evaluating every *other* kind of investment—and about evaluating the armies of people who are trying to sell you, whether sincerely or cynically, a dream and a sparkling return.

Summing Up:

1. We're drowning in information.
2. The goal: a simple and straightforward way to earn solid returns with the least possible risk.
3. Investor psychology is always at work behind the scenes, for each of us. Common sense and an approach that inspires high confidence are the antidotes.
4. The vehicle is important, but so is the driver.

chapter 1

THE FIRST HURDLE:
SAY GOODBYE TO BONDS
AND HELLO TO BOUNCING PRINCIPAL

The First Step

The first step for any successful investor is to understand the environment in which all investors must live. Just as nothing on Earth can be considered without considering gravity (which holds the Earth together), nothing in the world of investment can be considered without a focused awareness of the key forces which are always operating. In the previous chapter we discussed investor psychology—certainly one element that's constantly at work. We need to look at the more tangible financial factors as well.

The Silent March of Inflation

Perhaps because the monthly bill never arrives in the mail, most investors pay far too little heed to the basic underlying context in which their investments exist. That context is inflation. Since World War II there have only been two years in which inflation declined; the average annual inflation rate for the past sixty years has been 4.10%. And inflation compounds. As prices rise each year, the value of your original investment dollar declines.

Inflation marches on, quietly, rarely making headlines, and static dollars fall further and further behind.

Put simply, if prices double, the value of your investment must double merely to stay the same in terms of purchasing power—and that doesn't even begin to address the issue of having your money "go to work" for you, of getting a true investment return above the rate of inflation. And indeed, prices do double. At 4% inflation (lower than the long-term trend), prices double every 18.1 years. Think back. Twenty-five years back from this writing was 1980 (when inflation was above 10%, by the way). The cost of a new middle-of-the-line Ford was about $3,500 delivered. Today, that number is greater than $20,000. College tuitions have risen by nearly exactly the same amount. A new auto battery then cost $14, the same battery that today costs $70. In 1980 a cheap haircut cost $5. Today, even at the mall walk-in shops you'll have to pay $15–$20.

Since 1945, prices, as measured by the Consumer Price Index, have risen over 900%. Some prices have gone up even more. Health care costs rose over 200% in the decade of the 1980s alone, and continue to rise at roughly 9% per year. The "real" things we buy, such as a magazine, a paperback book, a slice of pizza, a movie ticket, a dental visit, a suit cleaning, etc. have risen two to three times as fast as the CPI in the past twenty years. Investors need to remember that in 1968 a gallon of gas cost about a quarter; as I write it is ten times that.

Chart 1 shows the "progress" of inflation since World War II. What it shows, very simply, is that if you could buy a product or service for $100 in 1945, by 2005 you would have to spend *$1,045.40* to get the same product or service. If your investments did not rise by over 1,000% during that period, you actually *lost* money, adjusted for inflation.

You might say that a loaf of bread in 1945 became a slice of bread by 2005, in terms of what you get for a depreciated dollar, or how many extra dollars you would need to account for increased costs. An automobile became a chassis and one tire. A whole hog became a several slices of bacon. A chandelier became a night light. Your $100,000 was transformed into just $9,563 of purchasing power by rising prices for everything.

So inflation is the context in which your investments exist, the starting point, the minimum benchmark against which investment performance must be measured. *The inflation rate is the first hurdle you must overcome.*

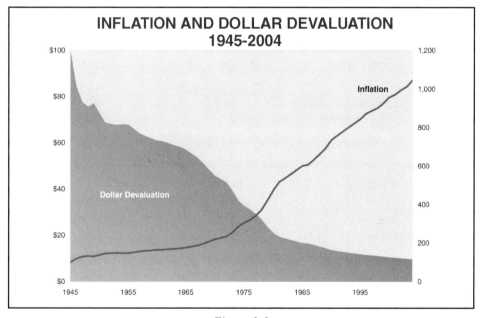

Figure 1-1

Why Fixed Income Investors Lose in the End

It's possible that during certain years the income a "T-Bill investor" earned was actually as high or higher than inflation. But consider what happens to the purchasing power of your income along the way, and, worse, the constantly shrinking real value of your principal.

Each year inflation takes its silent bite, and by the end of the period you can only buy a fraction of the goods and services you might have bought with your capital at the beginning of the period. Let's say you put away $10,000 in 1945 for your child's college. That might have seemed like a lot of money at the time and, indeed, you could have bought a small house with it. And let's say during the interim you spent the interest you received from a bond investment on extras like vacations or a second car payment. By the mid-sixties, when your child was ready to enter college, the annual cost for a private university was already $10,000 per year (I went to one that cost slightly more than that during the mid-sixties). The grand sum you saved for college would barely pay for one year after inflation had done its work!

Even at a moderate rate of 4% inflation (less than the post-World War II average) the value of money is cut by more than 50% in about a decade. For many key items, such as health care, it may be cut by more than half. Clearly, if you plan to live for more than ten years or so, your investment must rise enough to overcome the effects of inflation—and this is true of the income your investment produces if you need current income or will need the income later.

The nature of the economic environment leads to one inevitable conclusion: you cannot hide in fixed-income investments. So-called "safe" investments aren't safe at all when you realize that stagnant capital will not keep ahead of inflation. On the contrary, since we know that inflation exists, and since we know that bonds *do not* rise along with inflation, we know that bonds are actually *riskier* in the long term than investments which can increase in value.

Except for short-term parking of funds and to preserve fixed amounts that you may need in five years or less, all investors, whether they are retirees or corporate pension plans or churches or foundations, must say "goodbye to bonds," to T-bills, to bank C.D.s, to GIC's, to money market funds. For fixed-income investments are also fixed-principal investments, and the real value of your principal—as well as the real value of your "fixed" income— will diminish over time, like a vigorous man becoming frail and weak in old age.

The image in Chart 1-2 is something like the bible for professional investment advisors and students of investing. It shows the long-term return of various kinds of assets—T-bills, bonds, large stocks, small stocks—all as compared with inflation. Clearly, history has shown that stocks are far superior to fixed income (T-bills and bonds) when compared to inflation. And reason supports the view that this should be so. After all, investments in stocks are, theoretically at least, investments in something that grows, that gets larger. Investments in fixed income are investments in something that is intended to stay the same, something that's "fixed." One would expect stocks to do better, and history shows that they have, by a wide margin.

Bouncing Principal

But there's another big difference between stocks and fixed income. Stocks fluctuate in price. T-bills don't. Bonds fluctuate less than stocks (the shorter the time to maturity of a bond, the less it fluctuates in price). If you want the gains that stocks can provide, you've got to pay the toll. The toll is fluctuations. "Yeah, yeah, sure, sure, I know that!" say most investors. But you've got to do more than know it intellectually. You've got to accept it deeply, in your heart. You've got to embrace it—or your investment process will fall apart, done in by bad decisions and inadequate returns.

It's often said that everyone wants to get to heaven but no one wants to die. Investors, like everyone else who wants to reach a goal, have to pay a price. It's really not that difficult, once you realize that fluctuations are just a natural part of the process, a process that leads in laddered stair-steps to the heaven of solid investment returns. There's nothing wrong with an investment that fluctuates moderately, but their intolerance of fluctuations causes many overly cautious investors to pass up wonderful opportunities available to part-owners of sound and gradually growing businesses.

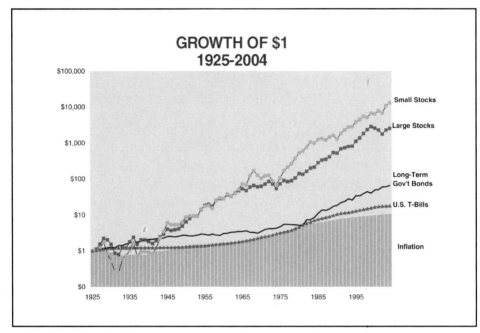

Figure 1-2

Note that there is no real competition between stocks and bonds over long term returns; stocks win mightily. Could this be caused by some odd period, some anomaly that appears in the middle of the data and produces a lopsided result when at most times the returns of bonds and stocks would be more similar? No way. Since 1926 (an eighty-year period) there have been fifty-nine twenty-year overlapping periods. In only one of those, the twenty-year period starting in 1929, did bonds manage to outperform stocks—and it was by less than 1 percentage point. In every other twenty-year period stocks outperformed bonds, through recessions and booms, war and peace, famine and pestilence, you name it. And they did so by a mile.

Let me put it bluntly, **bonds are a bad investment.** And they don't even do what most people think they do, which is provide a decent return with low volatility, as we shall see in the paragraphs upcoming.

Bonds, Bad

Bonds aren't investments, they're savings.

The important point here is that investors all too frequently buy bonds because they are "afraid" of the "market." This would be fine if bonds gave back a return that at least exceeded inflation, but not only do bonds underperform stocks, the <u>chances are high that in any given period bonds will not beat inflation</u>. In that case investor fears of the market are actually causing them to incur an inflation-adjusted loss. No one wants to invest for a loss, and if you're reading this book you're obviously seeking a better way. The path to a better way starts with the acceptance of the "bouncing principal" principle. You need to accept some risk—but that doesn't mean that you need to assume that risk is equal to loss. It's not.

Further, most people are still living in a sentimental past when it comes to understanding bonds and their market characteristics. You must bear in mind that until 1978, the Federal Reserve Bank tightly controlled interest rates nationwide. In 1978 however, the Fed decided to let interest rates float freely. Most observers see this as a distinct benefit to the economy, but look at this chart to see what the action did for the volatility of bond prices. As you can see, commencing from the date of "freedom," bonds became almost as volatile as stocks. Yet most people still think of bonds as in the old days, with low volatility. Yes, they're still less volatile, but just a pinch less so. Hardly enough to make up for the radical haircut you take when it comes to returns.

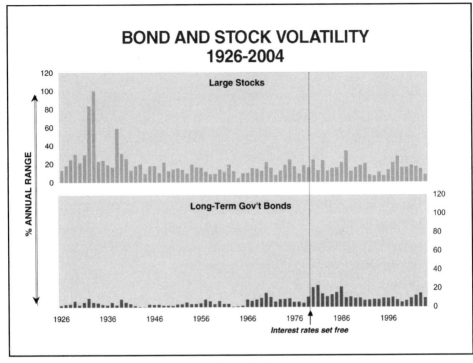

Figure 1-3

Learning to Love Fluctuations

With the correct perspective, one can learn to appreciate—and eventually seek out—investments that fluctuate (at least a little!). To be fair, a more volatile investment does harbor the possibility that it might be on a down-jump just when you need to sell because you need the money. In that case you would, in fact, lose money in an absolute sense, but it would have nothing to do with the intrinsic opportunities for that particular investment over the long term. What you should note about the volatility chart above, though, is that there's almost no substantive difference between bonds and stocks, yet we've already seen that stocks provide exponentially more reward.

There are, certainly, a few kinds of investment such as troubled companies, options and futures, or outright scams, where you can lose your money with no hope of ever getting it back. But in most cases, in most <u>reasonable</u> investments, we might say, the notion of risk is really more precisely a notion of *volatility*. That is, the value of the investment will fluctuate up and down—this is a given, based on the premise of an investment and the fact that an investment with no fluctuations can't be expected to generate an equal return to one that fluctuates. In theory, if "risk" is actually fluctuation, the *greater return* you get for investing in something with higher fluctuation is actually a kind of *payment for tolerating the fact that the value of your principal may bounce up and down.*

The return you earn is a "payment" for accepting the "bouncing principal," and it is also a payment for accepting the fact that you might need the money at a time of downward fluctuations.

In a real investment—as opposed to a speculation—your analytic process has already reduced the chances of permanent loss of some or all of your money to statistical unlikeliness. In other words, if you choose generic "growth stocks" or "index funds" as your investment, if you choose "real" investments with "investment quality" (as determined by the credit ratings agencies such as Standard and Poor's, for example), the issue of losing your money forever isn't really the right understanding of risk.

The right understanding of risk is an assessment of how often and how deeply the value of your investments will fluctuate, and whether you will be paid enough to accept that bouncing, compared to how much you get paid to accept the fluctuations in other investments. Most important, what are the *qualities* of the fluctuations and the *qualities* of the investments that are fluctuating, which affect how you *feel* about the fluctuations, which affect how well you are able to *tolerate* the fluctuations?

The Risk/Confidence Equation

Obviously, the right investment is going to have a *moderate magnitude of fluctuations relative to the return you can expect to get*. It is also going to have a moderate *quantity* of fluctuations relative to the return you can expect—it's not going to be jumping around *all the time*. But most important, the best long-term investment is going to be one where you have the *fullest faith and confidence* that it will fluctuate back up after it fluctuates down. That it will become more valuable over time.

Otherwise you'll be tempted to sell at the bottom out of fear, and your investment results will suffer. Indeed, the best long-term investment is the one that is easiest—from a psychological standpoint—to buy when the fluctuations have been down. In other words, one test of how good an investment is in terms of the ease of holding it, is to consider how attractive it may be to purchase or add more when its value has been decreasing.

When that is the test, and when that test has been passed, then you know you are talking about real investing—as opposed to swaying with whatever breeze happens to be passing at the moment. When your understanding of your investment is sufficiently great to overcome the natural fear that declining prices will persist forever, then you're no longer just a pawn of the great industry dedicated to selling investment products, you are actually an investor.

This is *not* to say that good investments must decline before they become interesting to buy: far from it. Many of the best stocks never really experience big or noteworthy declines. This, as they say late at night on TV, is merely a test. It's like a kind of litmus paper. If you feel so insecure about an investment that you'd be tempted to sell on a 10% or 20% decline, you need a better and more understandable investment, or an attitude adjustment, or both. (Hopefully, this book will fix both problems!)

Banks in the 1990s: A Case Study

I well remember the case against banks in 1990. Everything, in short, was wrong with banks. Interest rates were rising. Real estate loans were going into default across the country as fast as the lawyers could draw up the papers. Banks were getting stuck with property worth half the loan values, or less. Money market funds were attracting former bank depositors, offering higher rates, no early withdrawal penalties, and, horrors, free checking. Congress was threatening to break down the barriers between banks and brokerages, allowing both to perform normal banking functions as well as sell securities, and all the world knew that the securities firms would eat the banks' breakfasts, lunches, and dinners. The more the banks fell in price, the more investors thought they were terrible investments. The more they fell, the more intimations of bankruptcies and disasters were voiced by analysts at Wall Street firms. The analysts lowered their opinions to "hold" and "neutral" and "sell" with each new decline in share pricing. Banks were finally finished as an investment . . . forever(!).

Because the investment world could only think of reasons why banks would not "come back" as they have in the past, investors shunned them even after they reached almost absurdly low valuations. And all banks declined sharply, not just the handful that had serious problems. No one remembered that banks are the backbone of the economy, that the federal government had in the past and would always take extraordinary measures to preserve the viability of the banking system, that our economy overall is inconceivable without banks as the conduit of financial transactions. Nor was any credit given to bank managements for any ability at all to overcome their problems, though they had overcome problems many times in the past.

Because investors' *confidence level* about the long-term future of banks was thwarted by their negative attitudes, they only wanted to sell, and move to some safer shore. In other words, investors succumbed to the temptation to sell at the bottom and seek a situation where they could envision rising prices. They simply couldn't envision the upside when banks were falling like dominoes.

As we know today, however, since that decline banks have been among the *best* investments in the marketplace, *year after year*. The minority of cooler heads, who were able to see the contours of recovery in the longer term, weren't fazed by short-term problems, for short-term problems can beset any industry or company, and probably will, sooner or later. Since the banking crisis, though, many banks have tripled and quadrupled—all the while paying a hefty and rising dividend.

As prices decline, reasons for the decline always become apparent to all. The mass of investors grasp only the obvious, the present moment, and grasp it tightly. What people forgot to remember, though, were the many reasons why banks might rise again. It's a bit similar to the times when you're enraged at someone you've loved. In that heated moment, you forget the good parts.

Easy to Hold, Easy to Buy Declines

If you don't have faith that an investment will rise, tough times may prompt you to sell. Any investment that offers a threat to long-term confidence, that may be appealing to sell at the bottom rather than appealing to buy at the bottom, is not the right long-term investment. The right long-term investment will be, ironically enough, one that becomes more attractive to you as it declines. The opportunity to add more to your investment becomes as attractive as the actual gains you are seeking. From a psychological standpoint this will always be the best investment or investment strategy, because a *strong holder and one who can buy declines will always stand a better chance of success than one whose investment life is governed by the fear of loss.* Put another way, a good investment is one in which **paper** losses are tolerable.

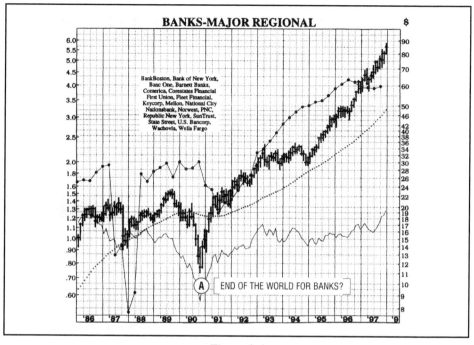

Figure 1-4

So the best long-term investment is one that is easy to hold, and easy to buy in moments of decline. An investment that's easy to hold and attractive to buy on declines must surely be one that inspires high confidence in the owner or buyer. High confidence must come from some mental process other than mere faith or infatuation, or it will not survive even the mildest of tests. The best long-term investment, then, has something about it which builds confidence in the long-term future—even though the current moment may include aspects that have frightened other investors.

But how do we find such investments? It's too vague to say there should be a good reward compared with the amount the investment fluctuates. We need to know how much reward is necessary for an adequate long-term investment. How much fluctuation needs to be tolerated, and how to get the least fluctuation for the most reward. But we don't need to get more than we need in an investment, and we certainly don't need to try to get more than the historical average. Reasonable goals are attainable. Fantasies are not.

Over the long term, conservative and careful investors are the ones still standing when the dust settles. Sometimes, when the latest new technology company is doubling and tripling overnight it may seem that you need to be an aggressive gambler, but these newsworthy moonshots are actually few and far between. More often than not, speculation will deplete your capital. Investors need to be willing to "take *human* bites," to seek gains that are commensurate with a moderate risk profile. Only a moderate risk profile will permit investors to attain the cool head and future-vision which is necessary to reach the *confidence level* that only *common sense* can bring. Too much or too little risk, and the brain just stops working.

Summing Up:

1. The first step in investing is to understand the environment, and the environment always includes inflation.
2. Over any extended period, prices rise and the value of a dollar declines. The inflation bill never arrives in the mail.
3. "Safe" investments such as T-Bills, Bonds, C.D.s, and money market funds are poor investments because what they give is less than inflation takes away.
4. History has shown that stocks are the right investment for an environment that includes inflation. Reason supports the historical record, since an investment in a business is an investment in something that grows.
5. Part of the "price" of having an investment that succeeds in our world is that it will fluctuate; we need to learn to tolerate the fluctuations. *Investments,* as opposed to "riskless" T-bills and C.D.s, will, as Bernard Baruch flatly noted, tend to fluctuate.

6. The true long-term investor will accept these fluctuations, and decide just how much "bouncing principal" is emotionally acceptable.
7. Conservative investors will seek investments that have an acceptable level of fluctuations, and are easy to hold or buy more of during periods of decline.
8. Your emotional relation—or, better yet, your *lack* of emotional relation—to your investment will make all the difference between good and bad decisions.

chapter 2

THE EIGHTH WONDER:
A FIRST LOOK AT COMPOUNDING

At the risk of sounding repetitive and boring, I'll say this again: the **Single Best Investment** strategy is not about "playing the market." It's about being a partner in an enterprise, and beyond that it's really about creating a kind of compounding machine that sits quietly off in the corner working for you while you go about your business. It's about harnessing the true power of time and growth, the incredible accumulation of modest gains into enormous ones which is the essence of compounding.

The gains are like bricks: you slowly and carefully place one atop the other. By and by—though not instantly—the shape of a building emerges. Once you've got a strong structure, the building can last many lifetimes, and you can furnish it with valuable antiques and art, or add rooms, or change around the partitions to make a new floor plan. Many people can't wait. They want to throw up a plywood pre-fab in a weekend. But that's like a shelter in a fable; in a strong wind there'll be nothing left save a pile of rubble.

However, the bricks of this compounding building aren't like the bricks you know. These bricks have the ability to generate new bricks, like a living thing. And these bricks can grow larger, like a living thing. And the bricks that they generate can grow larger, too. It is fecundity on earth, it is fruitfulness, it is multiplying, it is increase, it is like the universal process of cell division and proliferation that's ultimately behind the very creation of our bodies.

Compounding is the money that money makes, added to the money that money has already made. And each time money makes money, it becomes capable of making even more money than it could before! This is called a *virtuous circle*, and it's what we want to get working for us.

Simple Versus Compound Returns

Let's say I have $1,000, and I am able to achieve a return of 10% per year through investing it.

The **simple** return over ten years would be $1,000. I would receive $100 per year—10% of $1,000 for ten years, to reach the total of $1,000. If an investor pays $1,000 to buy a ten-year bond, for example, and receives $100 in interest each year, which she spends, she has received simple interest of 10% per year for ten years. At the end of that time, the investor has the original $1,000 (repaid when the bond matures) and now needs to look around for a new investment that, hopefully, will also pay 10% interest.

The **compound** return works differently. Here we assume that the money earned by the investment is **reinvested** in the same investment, rather than spent. In this case, after the first year the investor would have the original $1,000, plus an additional $100 (the earnings) generating returns.

Let's assume that all of the earnings could be reinvested at the same original rate. Over ten years the compounded return would look like this:

Table 2-1

END OF YEAR	REINVESTED CUMULATIVE TOTAL	SIMPLE CUMULATIVE TOTAL
1	$1,100	$1,100
2	$1,210 ($1,100+10% of $1,100)	$1,200
3	$1,331 ($1,210+10% of $1,210)	$1,300
4	$1,464	$1,400
5	$1,611	$1,500
6	$1,772	$1,600
7	$1,949	$1,700
8	$2,144	$1,800
9	$2,358	$1,900
10	$2,594	$2,000

Since the investor started with $1,000, the total gain for the ten years was $1,594, versus $1,000 in total earnings for the simple return. In other words, the reinvested, or *compounded* return was 59% higher.

Since as we know from the simple return example the actual earnings were $1,000, another way to look at this is to see that the *earnings* on the investment *earnings* earned 59%. This is what we mean by saying that money makes money, and that the money money makes, itself makes money. If you think of your capital as "working" for you, you can easily see that in a compounding situation you also get to have your capital's children working for you (and the children's children, and their children after that). Only in the world of pure investment, there are no child labor laws. You can work those little fellas twenty-four hours a day, and you should.

Here's what happens when the next generation kicks in:

Table 2-2

YEAR	REINVESTED CUMULATIVE	SIMPLE CUMULATIVE TOTAL
11	$2,853	$2,100
12	$3,138	$2,200
13	$3,452	$2,300
14	$3,797	$2,400
15	$4,177	$2,500
16	$4,595	$2,600
17	$5,054	$2,700
18	$5,560	$2,800
19	$6,116	$2,900
20	$6,727	$3,000
profit:	**$5,727**	**$2,000**
profit due to compounding:	**$3,727**	

After year 20, then, 10% annual gains compound up to $5,727 in *profits* (remember, we started with $1,000).

And what happens to the "simple" return investor? She earns another $100 per year, or $1,000 for the second ten years, or a total of $2,000 for the full twenty years. The actual profits attributable to compounding—remember, both approaches used an investment which returned 10% per year—were nearly three times greater in the reinvestment scenario. (And in one more year they would have been more than three times greater.) Bear in mind also that if inflation is 5% during this period, the "simple" investor's $3,000 at the end of the example would have experienced such an erosion in purchasing power that it would buy no more in real goods and services than the $1,000 she had in year one.

Compounding Magic

But the illustrations above are kind of small potatoes, since they cover a relatively short period of time. Here's what you'll find on the subject in *The Fundamentals of Corporate Science,* the basic textbook for the program leading to Certified Financial Analyst designation, a credential somewhat more prestigious than an MBA in today's finance world:

> The effect of compounding is not great over short time periods, but it really starts to add up as the horizon grows. To take an extreme case, suppose one of your frugal ancestors had invested $5 for you at [only] 6% interest 200 years ago. How much would you have today? The future value factor is a substantial $(1.06)^{200} = 115,125.91$, so you would have $5 x 115,125.91 = $575,629.53 today. Notice that the simple interest is just $5 x .06 = $.30 per year. After 200 years this amounts to $60. The rest is from reinvesting. Such is the power of compound interest.

An alert investor may now be thinking "but I need the income to live on, I can't just go and reinvest the earnings from my capital every year."

That's okay. Obviously, your long-term return on capital will be lower, but your life is your life, and there's nothing that can change that. What's intriguing about **Single Best Investment** stocks, though, is that you can still harness the power of compounding, even if you need to spend your income, because the stocks themselves benefit from compounding processes in the real world, and your capital can increase even if you're unable to reap all the benefits that reinvesting can bring.

Too, the magic of compounding can be felt on the *income* side of the ledger as well as in its effect upon principal. Your income can increase greatly through compounding even if you need to spend it—as long as it's in the right kind of stock. As you'll see in a few minutes, the right kind of stock can give you the kinds of increases in *income* that we saw in the tables above. Indeed, even if you're only concerned with income, you can wind up seeing your principal grow mightily, almost inadvertently, merely by focusing on investments that offer compounding income, income that rises.

Time is all you need. The effects of compounding increase markedly over time. Note that in our simple example at the end of the ten-year period compounded gains were $1,594 versus simple returns totaling $1,000, for a relative advantage 59 percentage points. But after twenty years the relative advantage of compounding increased to 372 percentage points (6,727 is 572% of 1,000, while $3000—the total of original principal plus simple interest— is 200% of 1,000). The difference only widens over time, and continues to widen as long as you continue to compound.

The reason is simple: each year your gains accrue to the principal amount that has increased in previous years, not just to the principal you started out with. When your principal has increased tenfold, for example, it takes only a 1% gain to generate the same amount of profit (in dollars) as would have required a 10% gain on your original capital.

Compounding is really one of the great processes on earth, and it's given free to all who care to participate in it. Unfortunately, few do. As capital builds up, there's almost inevitably a use found for it, or a clever heir who manages to get his or her hands on it. Indeed, here's another intriguing yet arithmetically unassailable example from *The Fundamentals of Corporate Science:*

In 1626 Peter Minuit bought all of Manhattan for about $24 in gold and trinkets from the Native Americans who lived there. This sounds cheap, but the Indians [sic] may have gotten the better end of the deal. To see why, suppose the Indians had sold the goods and invested the $24 at 10%. How much would it be worth today, 365 years later?

The future value is . . . roughly 31.2 quadrillion dollars.

Well $31.2 quadrillion is a lot of money. How much? If you had it, you could buy the United States. All of it. Cash. With money left over to buy Canada, Mexico, and the rest of the world for that matter.

This example is something of an exaggeration. In 1626 it would not have been easy to locate an investment that would pay 10% every year without fail for the next 365 years.

And, I might add, it would also be extremely difficult to avoid dipping into the pot for a new Jaguar from time to time.

Compounding has nearly turned staid men into chirping poets:

Baron Rothschild said "I don't know what the seven wonders of the world are, but I know the eighth, compound interest." Albert Einstein found in compounding the same kind of almost mysterious universal energy that he had sought in relativity physics, calling it, "the greatest mathematical discovery of all time." And as Benjamin Franklin's famous Poor Richard aptly put it, "I never saw an oft removed tree/ That throve so well as those that settled be."

Balancing Compound Returns and Volatility

All investments that make use of compounding returns and the compounding principle are not created equal, though sometimes the distinctions are not easy to make. If compounding alone were the issue, we could determine which stocks have the highest end-point return, assert that the future will be like the past, and just invest in those past winners. Sadly, the world is not that neat.

Be sure to note that the long-term return numbers for stocks or mutual funds that you hear bandied about are *compounded* average annualized returns. What does this mean?

Clearly, no investment that fluctuates has the same return each year over a long period, though you'll hear that this fund had a return of 15.6% for the past five years, or this index returned 12% over the past ten years. The return is not the average of the simple returns over a period, either. It is the cumulative total return (the growth of a dollar, in other words) for the period divided by a factor which tells you what the annual return *would have been had it been the same each year,* in order to reach the same cumulative return.

In other words, if an investment gained 200% over twenty years, the average annual compound return (also called the time-weighted return) is not merely 200% divided by 20% or 10%. There is a formula which tells us what the average gain would have had to be for the twenty years in order to arrive at 200% as a total gain. In this case, the average annual compound return needed was only 5.65%. (The formula—which you don't really need to know—is as follows: $FV=PV(1+r)^N$ years where FV equals future value, PV equals present value, r equals interest, and ^{N} equals number of compounding periods.)

In order to truly compare two different investments, you need to know the volatility of each. You want to know how much compound return can be

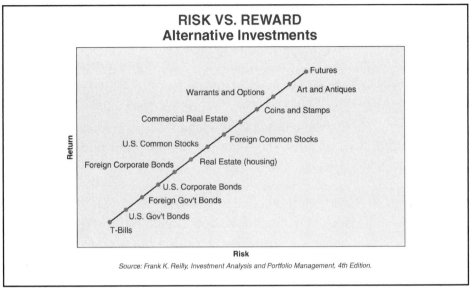

Figure 2-1

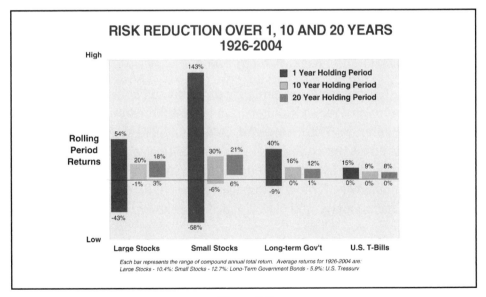

Figure 2-2

expected per unit of risk, per unit of fluctuation. This is often measured by what's called standard deviation. Standard deviation is basically a number that tells you if the investment is more bouncy or less bouncy, on its way to the final cumulative return. If investment A returns 200% and has a standard deviation of 9, it has got to be more attractive than investment B which returns 200% but has a standard deviation of 15. Both give you the same ultimate result, but investment A does it with a much "smoother ride," with less fluctuations. (See Figure 2-1). And time smooths your ride as well (See Figure 2-2).

The game, then, for all but the greediest investors, is simple: find the best return with the lowest standard deviation. Find the best *risk-adjusted* compound average annual returns. There's often but not always a trade-off in accepting lower returns for lower volatility. And this is what's made the quest for the **Single Best Investment** so fascinating. Where can you find the best balance of high compound average annual returns and low average annual volatility? Obviously, I think it's the strategy outlined in the following pages.

Time, Patience, and the Right Kind of Stock

It's not enough, in my view, to simply try for gains and hope they compound well enough to provide, ultimately, an inflation-beating result. That's only playing offense. What's needed is a total investment process that harnesses the power of compounding in a positive way, that's pervaded by compounding, that uses the compounding principle to create value in a multi-dimensional way. A process that uses compounding intrinsically—not just after the fact to arrive at a performance calculation.

This is what's different about SBI stocks. Here, rather than "playing the market" to arrive at a return, we make use of the "inner compounding" that operates within a specific group of stocks to create an investment portfolio that has an actual, rational, projected return. An inevitable return, you might say, despite the uncertainties and equally inevitable ups and downs of the environment within which it exists.

Time is a crucial element. Every successful investor will sooner or later come to the eternal verity that in this area of life, "time is your friend." In a sense, when you understand the impact of time on compounding, you understand that investing is a kind of discipline, a kind of spiritual path (ironically enough) to teach you patience.

Recall the table in the beginning of this chapter. In the first few years, there's not a heck of a lot of difference between simple returns and compound returns. It's there, but it doesn't seem to have much impact as a percentage of invested capital. After all, in year 5 the compounding side shows only a little more than $100 superiority over simple returns. That's something, and it's certainly 10+% more than simple returns, but it hardly seems worth striking up the band and proclaiming the "eighth wonder of the world." No, the matter only gets serious as time passes, and as the *returns earned on prior returns* begin to build. It creeps up on you, just like inflation creeps up on you. It's a quiet process, and it needs time to incubate.

We'll talk more about time later on. For now, remember: time is on your side in the right investment situations. The corollary is obvious: you must give a compounding program time to do its job. If the notion of compounding holds only one lesson it is this: the first prerequisite for successful investing is patience. If you think you don't have patience, begin a process of developing it. Look into your heart and find out why you're in a rush. Understand yourself, and try to make contact with that part of you that *is* patient: it's a part we all have.

Think of anything you've done over a long period of time, whether it's a skill or a relationship or a hobby or even just living. You're probably a lot better at it and you probably know a lot more than you did when you started. This is the effect of compounding. This is the cumulative return.

It's not very different in investing. The real difference is that you must learn to be passive. That is, after all, the definition of an investor: a passive part-owner of a business, a shareholder. The trick is simple: find a business with *reliable growth that will share that growth with its owners, be patient and watch it grow.* Fast growth is not the goal, for fast growth is not reliable growth and isn't worthy of your patience. *Reliable* growth, no matter how modest, is what will reward you in the end. Long-term, the business in which you have invested will experience a compound growth of its own, and you will be a part of it.

Summing Up:

1. It's not about playing the market, it's about becoming a partner in a business.
2. Compounding is a building with bricks which themselves make bricks.
3. Even annual returns of 10% can produce gains of nearly 600% in twenty years.
4. Time is all you need. Time and a sensible investment that makes maximum use of compounding.

chapter 3

THE SINGLE BEST INVESTMENT: CREATING YOUR OWN PRIVATE COMPOUNDING MACHINE

We're heading toward a goal: to actually **be** an investor, to stop "playing the market," to stop trying to guess what group or style will be best in the next cycle, to take action that won't have to be undone in a few months' time, to get the benefits of investing in equities without running the gauntlet of anxieties.

There is, in fact, a way to accomplish this. My real-time experience, the experience of many great investors, and the teachings of virtually every academic study confirm it is so. The way to do it is to build *your own private compounding machine*. You build it using good "parts" that are in fine working order, you maintain it as needed with an occasional lube and oil change, and you leave it alone—you let the machine do its job.

Components of the Machine

In the preceding chapters we've reviewed most of the "parts" of this machine:

First, we looked at the personal, emotional situation of the investor, the "operator" of any system or strategy. The world of investing is dynamic and often unpredictable, forcing investors into what are often emotional reactions to events—even though the investor may experience his or her behavior as rational and logical. We aren't up against the mere roar of change and the simple cacophony of experts intent upon separating us from our money or simply bolstering their own egos. We're up against ourselves, with all our frailties, foolishness, foibles, and naiveté. Any strategy (or "machine") must include in its design a recognition of humanness, and try to provide a kind of exclusion of the self.

Second, we reviewed the notion that in the long-term economic environment which faces all investors, growth of both principal and income are essential. Fixed income cannot be a part in the machine. Fixed income simply doesn't provide good enough returns to overcome inflation plus provide additional solid real returns to justify the inherent risks and volatility.

Third, the compounding machine must really focus on the miracle that compounding truly is. That means income is reinvested whenever possible (as you'll see, you can still have a compounding machine and withdraw income, it just won't be as effective as one that reinvests), and it also means that an investor's most powerful tools are time and patience. A broad, panoramic view is needed: an obsession with monthly or quarterly returns will simply gum up the gears.

Fourth, the compounding machine should make use of the investment areas that show the highest risk-adjusted returns, the biggest return per unit of risk. Historic results combined with reason have shown us the path to the right stocks for use in building our machine. These "right" stocks must also be easy to hold, for we know that the biggest pitfall for investors are the problems and bad decisions that arise from the anxiety of holding stocks through the ups and downs of "bouncing principal."

Dividend Growth Is the Hidden Key

But there's one feature of the stocks we want to use we haven't discussed yet, and it is the hidden key to the Single Best Investment. A moment's reflection will confirm for you that this is an absolutely powerful secret, and yet there are very few investors actually using it. If this were not the case, if this factor were in widespread use, you would see a nation of happy investors whistling their way toward retirement. But you don't. All you see are nervous nellies, checking the price of the Dow Jones daily and intra-day, scanning the most-actives list for some key to the future, subscribing to the newsletters filled with hyperbole and sketchy research, breathlessly hanging on every word of some smug talking head on the business news channel.

This hidden key is, in a simple phrase, **dividend growth.**

As we know, mature companies pay dividends from their earnings. Every quarter the company sends a check to investors, sharing a small fraction of the profits, and many investors love those checks. The feature that few have heeded, though, is that a significant number of companies *raise their dividend every year* (or nearly every year). To most, this seems merely a nice amenity, but because most people don't have a long-horizon worldview, they totally underestimate the potency of this factor. It is, in fact, the electricity that will make your compounding machine run. It's the gas for your engine. Dividend growth is the critical piece in the puzzle for creating a portfolio that will serve you over the years.

Pay attention. This is a simple idea, but it is also the single most important idea for long-term investors. The reason it is so important is that *dividend growth drives the* *compounding principle* for individual stocks in a way that is certain and inevitable. It is an authoritative force that compels higher returns regardless of the other factors affecting the stock market.

Let's say you have two bonds with equal credit ratings and equal time to maturity. Bond A pays you $100 per year and bond B pays you $200 per year. Which bond will have a higher price? Of course bond B will sell for twice the price of bond A, at which point they will both offer the same percent yield. The important point is that *an instrument that produces income is valued based on the amount of income it produces.* And if it produces more income, it is worth more. The same would be true for, say, an apartment building—the more income it produces, the higher the market value. Or a hardware store—again, the more income, the more an owner could get for the store if he wanted to sell the business.

What makes rising income that comes from a growing dividend so attractive in a yield stock? You not only receive greater income as the years go by, you also get a rising stock price—because **the instrument producing the income (the stock) is worth more as the income it produces increases.** In effect, you get a "double dip" when you invest in high-yield stocks that have rising dividends. You get the *income that increases* to meet or surpass inflation, and you get the *effect of that rising income* on the stock price, which is to force the stock price higher.

That last paragraph has phrases in bold and phrases in italics, and some phrases are underlined. These are for emphasis. If I could get words to jump off the page and pull on your sleeves or tweak your nose, I would. But I'm stuck with words, so the least I can do is suggest that you read the last paragraph again, and remember it, and remember it well. And I can repeat, and repeat, so you don't forget: **you get rising income, and the increasing income makes the stock that's producing that income increasingly valuable.**

Dividends Tell the Truth

Dividends and dividend growth are the real-life signal that a company has the wherewithal to pay you dividends, that it has your interests at heart in the fact that it pays you dividends, and that it is experiencing real growth as proven by the real growth in its real dividends.

Bear in mind that we're not dealing here with some financial trick or some ponzi scheme run by unscrupulous corporations intent on boosting the price of their stock. On the contrary, the very attention we place on rising dividends puts us squarely in the position of "owners" of a company, of true investors who understand that a satisfying and reasonable return from a stock investment isn't a gift of the market or luck or the consequence of listening to some market maven, but *it is the logical and inevitable result of investing in a company that is actually doing well enough, in the real world, to both pay dividends and to increase them on a regular basis*.

Dividends are paid from earnings. When a company has reached a certain level of maturity and stability, it begins paying dividends, not unlike the way in which an individual begins saving once she's reached a level of income that satisfies her basic needs.

But many companies perceive an *earnings* report as an opportunity for "creative accounting." Sales can be booked early or late. Liabilities are written off right away or amortized. Contracts might be recorded as immediate income or only as and when paid. Capital asset sales are sometimes deemed ordinary income. There are a million ways for companies to "look good" at earnings time, in hopes of supporting their stock prices. Don't forget, a huge share of corporate executives' compensation, and often their very jobs, are dependent on either meeting their earnings objectives or increasing the stock price, or both. So companies have a big incentive to "put their best foot forward."

That's why dividends are a kind of acid test or litmus paper that reveals the true state of a company's finances. As Geraldine Weiss so aptly observed, "dividends don't lie." In order for a company to pay a dividend, it must have the money to pay it with. Earnings can't be some accounting sleight-of-hand. They must actually be there, in cash. Thus, while we as passive investors can never know as much about the companies we invest in as we'd like, we can know one thing: if a company pays a dividend it has the cash with which to pay that dividend.

Further, a company that raises its dividend is truly *signaling* the state of its business to investors. Picture a boardroom, and the classic board of directors' table filled with wizened business people, people who know that there are fads and fashions and cycles, and things can go up and down, and even go bump in the night. These directors know just how well their company is doing or how poorly. They know how much will be needed to fund capital expansion or research and development, or the next takeover. They know the whole financial picture, and they also know that dividend reductions are death to stock prices. The one thing a board *never* wants to do is *decrease* the dividend, so increasing a dividend is a clear statement that the company's fortunes are positive—or at least positive enough to keep paying and to raise the dividend.

In other words, a company can *tell* you about its earnings, but there is always a certain "flexibility." There is no flexibility when it comes to paying and increasing dividends. The company must have the cash to pay to you.

What you see is what you get. Through the dividend, a company can **show** you how well it's doing.

So dividends are real, like the income from an apartment building or a liquor store or a bank CD. And dividend growth is real. Neither dividends nor dividend growth are some propaganda from the company, nor some hype from a brokerage firm or newsletter writer, nor some error in judgment by a finance magazine.

This is a good thing, for we wouldn't want to build our compounding machine on a foundation of chimera and public relations ploys. We want our parts to be real, working, brand-name, durable.

Indeed, a 2004 paper by A. Koch and A. Sun of Carnegie Mellon University suggested, with a batch of interesting statistics, that investors bought dividend growth stocks not for the signal that management was providing about the future, but because the dividend growth confirmed what management had already reported about the past. In these days of aggressive CEOs and accounting at many firms, consideration of dividend growth as a kind of litmus test of previously reported earnings is not a trivial feature. Take your pick: a signal about future prospects or a verification of past reports—in either case it's bottom-line valuable information available nowhere else about your investment.

Dividend Growth as a "Part" in the Machine

Now back to dividend growth as the driver, the energizing force, of the compounding machine. Let's look first at just the _income_ side of the ledger, and what consistent dividend increases do to your position as an investor.

As I write, the dividend yield on the S&P 500 is about 1.6%, and the current dividend yield for one of my firm's managed portfolios is about 4.5%. (We manage four types of individual portfolios for private and institutional investors, with varying yields.) So let's take a theoretical stock (we'll examine plenty of real stocks later on) from the broad market portfolio with a current yield of 4.5%. At this moment there are plenty of fine companies with current yields that are higher, and plenty with yields that are a bit lower, though we'd rarely consider one with a yield as low as the current S&P 500. So we'll go with the "average" of our holdings. Too, the average of our holdings shows a projected dividend growth of 10% per year, so we'll plug in that number as well. That's higher than the market, but not too high considering that a company need only grow its earnings by 10% per year in order to raise the dividend 10% and still pay out the same portion of its earnings in dividends.

We buy, in this theoretical or "average" world, a stock—we'll call it LM Corp.—which offers a current yield of 4.5% and a projected dividend growth of 10%. In this case the company is projected to grow its earnings by 15% per year, so our 10% per year dividend growth assumption seems fairly conservative. To make matters easy, let's assume that the stock sells for $100 and pays a dividend of $4.50 per year (a quarterly dividend of $1.125).

After one year, the dividend is raised by 10%, to $4.95 ($4.50 + 10% of $4.50 or $.45, added to last year's dividend of $4.50). Does this cause our stock price to jump higher, because the yield is higher? Maybe, maybe not. It depends to some extent on the nature of the market, the stocks which are presently in vogue, and what has happened to interest rates over the past year. In fact, one year's dividend growth is not going to make much of a difference. In that way, dividend growth is like inflation. No one pays much attention to it in terms of their present decisions until it has built up to a level that sets off an emotional or tangible alarm. One year's dividend growth doesn't ring the investors' greed bell, you might say.

In year two, the dividend is raised by 10% again, this time rising to $5.445 (last year's $4.95 + 10% of $4.95 or .495, equaling $5.445). Is our stock up yet? Maybe, maybe not. But one thing is sure. You've received your dividends and you're now receiving a 5.45% return on your *original* investment—probably better than a bank C.D. or a money market fund. And it goes on like this:

Table 3-1

Year	Dividend yield return on <u>original</u> $100 investment
3	$6.00
4	$6.59
5	$7.25
6	$7.98
7	$8.78
8	$9.65
9	$10.62
10	$11.67

(dollars and cents return equals percentage yield on $100 investment)

By year seven (halfway through the year) we see that return on original investment **from dividends alone** is about 9%. Many investors may not be aware that the long-term *total* returns—dividends plus stock price increases—from stocks during most of the twentieth century has been about 11%, and about 12% since World War II (but the 11% figure is the one most commonly used by academic scholars of finance and institutional pension funds, and by consultants who are in the business of having reasonable expectations about investment returns). During year 9 we're going to hit that 11% figure *from dividends alone!* And the income isn't going to fluctuate up and down like the market, it's only going to fluctuate up, as your dividends continue to increase!

Send your mind out even further in time. The further out you go, the greater the impact of compounding. Let's say you continue to increase dividends at 10% per year for another seven years. At that point your yield (on your original investment) from income alone will have reached 18%–20% per year. That's double the expected average annual total returns from stocks, and it will continue, increasing each year on and on and on into the indeterminate future. If you think you can find a mutual fund that will offer you those kinds of returns over a long period—and deliver on the promise—you ought to check and see if your health plan covers psychiatric care and mental incapacity!

Time Is on Your Side

We used a hypothetical example, but this principle is not hypothetical. At our firm we have clients who come to us with portfolios stuffed with General Electric or Exxon or Merck purchased in the fifties and sixties. And the current income from these positions is often 100% or more of the original investment cost. Often these clients don't want to sell for fear of paying taxes. But I tell them not to sell for a different reason: they did the right thing already once, why tempt the fates? Basically, if you'd like to have an annual income equal to your investment capital, all you have to do is buy the right stocks and sit on them. Compounding dividends will do the rest. In a hurry? We might be able to speed up the process a bit through buying stocks especially selected to play an active part in the compounding machine. In any case, if you want the end result you've got to give it time. Can you be satisfied with a 20% annual return that rises even higher every year, a return you can actually put in your pocket without spending principal? You can get there in less than two decades . . . if you stick to the program.

But that's only half the story. Less than half, in fact.

Rising Dividends Create Rising Prices

In our LM Corp. example we asked, during the initial periods, "is the stock up yet?" "Is the stock up yet?" (If that sounds like a kid wanting to stop on the highway for ice cream it's no accident. Infantile wishes for sweets and instant gratification don't go away just because you've lived a certain number of years and have enough money to invest in corporate stock.) After year one or year two or year three, it's hard to say exactly when the pressure of a higher yield alone begins to force the stock price upward. One would presume that the stock would be treated well in the marketplace because it was at least doing well enough to raise its dividend, and that's usually the case, though there's no guarantee, of course.

Sooner or later, assuming roughly "normal" price/earnings multiples and interest rates, and roughly "normal" oscillations in investor preferences for different kinds of stocks, the value of the increased income of your stock *must* push up the price of the stock that produces the income. For stocks compete not only with each other for investors' dollars, they also compete with interest rate instruments. Sooner or later, even if the market hates this particular company—which is highly unlikely if it sports a record of both earnings growth and dividend growth—it will rise as it becomes more attractive than other kinds of income-producing instruments such as bonds.

In fact, all things being equal, a perfect-world result is simple to divine: **the stock will rise as much as its dividend income rises.** If the income doubles, the stock should double, roughly speaking. If the income goes up 50%, the stock price should follow. In other words, that stock whose income return on original investment rose fourfold to 18% in fourteen years would also rise fourfold in price—pushed up by the value of its rising stream of income.

One may argue that this is all very theoretical, but the real-world concurrence with the principle involved is simply uncanny. In most cases, stocks rise at least in tandem with the rise in their income, sometimes much higher than that (when the market decides the stock has been "undervalued" and investors don't require such a high yield in order to buy it, or when the consistency of growth becomes so attractive that investors are willing to pay more for it). We'll look at many examples later on.

We've seen that compounding in stocks has an amazing effect when given some time to work. But compounding with reinvested dividends has an *astronomical effect* over time. It turns out, according to Ibbotson and a number of subsequent studies which have followed in his footsteps, that dividends are the single most important factor in long-term compounded returns (remember, they are always positive, each and every quarter). According to the *Stocks, Bonds, Bills, and Inflation 1997 Yearbook* published by Ibbotson Associates:

> "One dollar invested in large company stocks at year-end 1925, with dividends reinvested, grew to $1,828.33 by year-end 1996: this represents a compound annual growth rate of 11%. Capital appreciation alone caused $1.00 to grow to $58.07 over the 72-year period, a compound annual growth rate of 6.2%. Annual returns ranged from a high of 54% in 1993 to a low of -43.3% in 1931. The average annual dividend yield was 4.6%."

Call me crazy, but it would appear that Ibbotson attributes over 97% of the long-term total return from stocks to dividends and their reinvestment in more shares (price change alone was 97% of the total with dividends reinvested). The difference in return between stocks without dividends and stocks with dividends is as vast as the difference between the total returns of stocks and bonds.

Ask any financial professional how much of total returns from stocks is attributable to dividends, and they'll tell you "about half." Which isn't so far from right, since as we saw above, the average dividend yield was a bit less than half of the annual total return of 11%. But they forget that the dividend gets reinvested in more shares, which themselves are increased by total return, and which themselves yield dividends to be invested in yet more shares. Soon you have two shares for every one that you started with, then three, then four. And on and on, ashes to ashes, dust to dust.

To see the relationship between time and the compounded growth of dividends, take a look at the pro forma results of normal arithmetical compounding over a more "human" and conceivable time frame of twenty years, without any special "good things" happening to a stock. We prepared the following chart to illustrate the difference between a rising dividend investment and a fixed income investment, using market rates and our high-yield portfolio rate at the end of 1997.

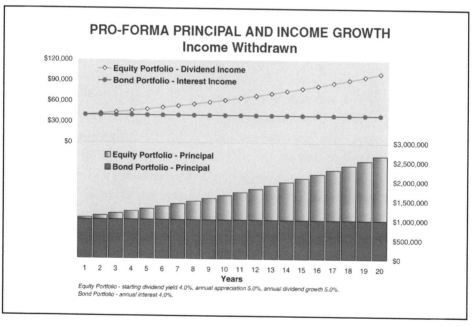

Figure 3-1

This chart shows what your position would be if you simply withdrew income at the end of each year. What you see is simply the growth of the income return, and the capital appreciation of the stock.

1. Total income was $2,242,081 over twenty years, based on an initial investment of $1 million.
2. Total appreciation was $2,207,135 over the same twenty years, based on that same $1 million initial investment (Remember, it is assumed that the stocks you owned would appreciate in an amount at least equal to the dividend growth).
3. By the end of year 20, you would have an annual return of $184,410 or 18.4% from income alone (the percent return is based on your original investment).
4. By the end of year 20 your stock value would have grown from $1 million to $3,207,135—excluding the $2,242,081 in income withdrawn.

Your total return, based on simply adding the total income to the total principal gain, would have been just about 445%. Calculated as an average annualized return, the number would be 12.1%. Bear in mind that by year 20 your return from income alone at over 18%, even if you spent all the income every year and didn't reinvest, would be higher than the average total return from stocks (income plus appreciation) during one of the best periods in history, and that return will only increase as the dividends rise. Note that if you were stuck in fixed income, your annual yield would still be the same as it was, at 5.5% or $55,000 per year.

But this doesn't tell you your return had you reinvested all dividends in more stock (using the theoretical average stock price for the year)—and as we know from Ibbotsen, it is the reinvestment of income that really powers up long-term returns. In the next chart we see the effects of reinvestment in the same return scenario. Because you reinvest, everything increases exponentially.

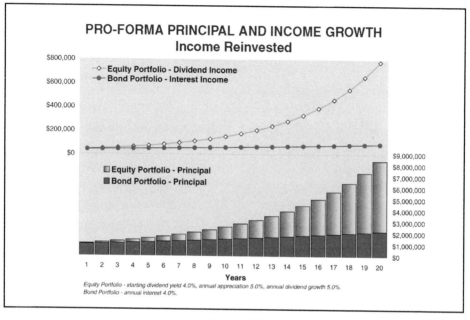

Figure 3-2

Over the same twenty years, based on the same $1 million investment, this time:

1. Total income received was $4,440,234.
2. Total appreciation was $8,277,788.
3. By the end of year 20 you'd have annual income of $533,472 from income alone. That's a 53% return on your original investment, each year, every year, from income only.
4. Your total return in the reinvestment scenario is 1,271%.

All this, for a little patience and discipline, and the willingness to have faith in the early years, when the power of compounding is not so obvious.

The reinvestment plan works so well because you are continually buying more shares, and those shares themselves reap both income and capital gains.

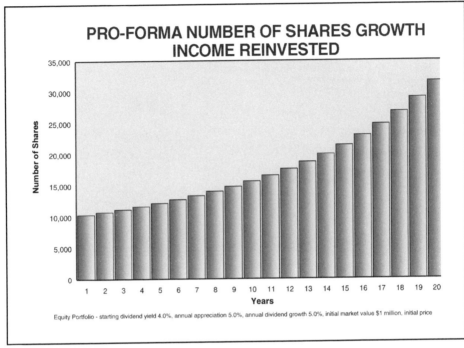

Figure 3-3

Note the "# of shares" column. This is increased each year by the amount of income that is available to purchase more shares. The income available to purchase more shares is itself a function of the number of shares held. The "machine" purrs and purrs this way, with no discernible end-point. At the 20 year mark, for example, we now have 2.76 shares for each share purchased initially. This also means that for every one percent gain in the stock(s) initially purchased, the investor will now experience a 2.7% gain on original investment. Nifty.

As you can see, the Single Best Investment approach—a conservative and easygoing strategy—harnesses a hidden power that is far more effective than the prognostications of any market guru or short-term stockpicker. If all goes according to plan, it is possible for you to equal or exceed the returns of even the best investors. But as you can also see, time and patience are the keys, and few investors, constantly bombarded by the opinions of pundits and friends and manipulative salespeople, can stick to such a plan long enough for it to pay its luscious "dividends." But the rewards are there if you've got the discipline.

Times change. There are better and worse periods for every kind of strategy, and sometimes even the best returns are only mediocre compared to the salad days of, say, the mid-1990s. But, even if you run into a slow period for the market the relative returns—returns compared to other strategies—are sure to stand head and shoulders above the pack. It must be so, for eventually *the income portion alone is more than most investors in most other strategies will realize,* and it is inconceivable that such a radical increase in income will not eventually produce an increase in the value of the assets producing the income. It is frankly, difficult to even find a single example of a stock that did not rise if its income started from a reasonably high base and rose substantially over a period of several years.

Finally, investors should surely bear in mind, amidst all this discussion of fabulous returns, that the Single Best Investment approach is probably **the most conservative and risk-averse** strategy that you can possibly use to invest in the long-term growth of the economy and the corporate stocks within that economy. It is an approach that's easy to comprehend and easy to stay with—once you comprehend that you're a partner in a business and that all good things take time to develop.

If you're a "steady-eddie" investor, or you want to become one, turn now to the next chapter. In it I'll detail the exact criterion to look for in a Single Best Investment stock. The selection process isn't hard, and there are shortcuts and rules of thumb for those who don't want to add the understanding of balance sheets and income statements to their array of skills. But you should learn the important basic parameters and avoid straying from them.

There will be plenty of stocks to choose from, in a variety of industries, and all of them will fit the profile we've established as stocks in which *long-term compounding of the company's profits, manifested to you through rising dividends, is the key principle that will translate into long-term compounding of your returns as an investor.* Indeed, when you think about it, how could it be any other way?

Summing Up:

1. Create a compounding machine, don't play the market.
2. The operator is just as important as the machine.
3. Dividend growth is the energy that drives the compounding machine.
4. Dividend growth is the true signal of a prospering company.
5. Dividend growth pushes up the price of a stock.
6. Stock prices should theoretically rise in a percentage increment equal to the amount of dividend growth (applies to stocks with above-average yields).
7. Reinvestment brings you more and more shares, each of which earns dividends and is subject to the effects of dividend growth.

chapter 4

THE SINGLE BEST INVESTMENT STRATEGY APPLIED

How do you pick a Single Best Investment stock? First, you need to learn how to recognize potential candidates, a formula we'll cover in this chapter. In subsequent chapters we'll look at more specific tools for determining relative value and outline a process for choosing between candidates. Throughout, bear in mind that the Single Best Investment approach relies on a simple formula, so simple it almost seems impossibly simple:

> **High quality**
> **+ High _current_ dividend**
> **+ High _growth_ of dividend**
> _____
> **= High total returns**

Everything we require of a stock is geared to fulfilling that formula. And, if a stock doesn't qualify under the simple formula above, we don't want it.

THE COMPONENTS OF HIGH QUALITY

What's high quality? High quality stocks have superior financial strength, as signaled by low debt, strong cash flow, and overall creditworthiness. High quality companies have proven their staying power through good and bad times, with strong and creative management, proven products, and a proven market for those products.

Financial Strength

Financial strength is the key requirement of a high-quality stock. After all, a business is a financial entity, no matter what business it is in nor what management philosophy it uses to implement its business plan. Remember, you're buying a piece of a business here, one that you want to live with for a long, long time.

Low debt. The first item that indicates financial strength is low debt. You want a company that's able to make money without heavy financing needs. When companies need lots of borrowing to keep a business afloat, they also take on important vulnerabilities. If sales slow down—and there are always slow periods, even for the most stable and reliable businesses—heavy borrowers face the issue of being able to make their interest payments. Since the business can be lost entirely if loan payments aren't made, they naturally assume the highest priority in a company's expenditures. This means other aspects of the business may suffer: marketing, research and development, retaining valuable employees, making capital investments— all the things that keep a business moving forward and keep it a step ahead of the competition. Companies that need to borrow heavily may also have to borrow when rates are high, building in a fixed cost that may be greater than the business can easily bear. Worst of all, interest payments have a higher priority than dividends, and if cash flow declines to the point where dividends can't be raised, or have to be cut or eliminated (perish the thought!), you've got a wrench in the gears of your compounding machine instead of a smoothly functioning "part."

Selected utilities and a handful of other companies whose cash flow is maximally predictable and steady can afford as much as roughly half debt and half equity in their capitalization (a very few, even more). Capitalization is the total of debt and stock, and the usual term for evaluating how heavily a company has borrowed is the debt/capitalization or the debt/equity ratio. Half debt and half equity would give you a debt/capitalization of 50%. Except in specific cases we'll be discussing later, your company **should not have a ratio of more than 50%.** In other words, it should not have—unless there is a compelling reason to make an exception—more debt than equity. For our purposes, in our specific strategy, the less debt the better. (See Appendix B for more on debt levels related to specific types of companies, and Appendix C includes sources for information).

Another and perhaps more practical way of looking at debt levels is called the "coverage." You want to know the relationship of a company's gross profit to the amount it must pay in debt. If gross profits (profits from sales after deducting administrative and general expense and taxes) provide ample coverage of the debt, and if those gross profits are predictable and reliable, you need be less concerned about the absolute level of debt. Look for coverage of at least 3:1 to insure financial strength. That is, the **cash flow of the company after taxes is at least three times the amount of interest it pays.** There are plenty of rules of thumb, but the best *attitude* is to avoid going up to the limit. Let coverage be as ample as possible.

Some economists might assert that a company should have some debt, for reasons we need not delve into now, but for our purposes no debt is better than some debt, and less debt is better than more debt. Bear in mind that one of our key goals is to find an investment that's easy to hold; we don't want to be forced out of an investment by anxiety when times are difficult. When times are tough, it's rather more comfortable to be an owner of a business with no debt than an owner of a business that's beholden to banks and bondholders. (Again, there's more information on exceptions in Appendix B.)

Strong cash flow. When times are tough, the financially strong and financially flexible companies (strong companies have the flexibility to take advantage of opportunities that arise) actually grow stronger. They're able to buy competitors that falter, choked by excessive financing and inadequate cash flow. They're able to take market share by beefing up marketing just when their competitors are forced to retrench. They can afford to buy the best talent if that's what's needed. They can develop new products that will make a long-term difference.

Financial strength means more than that a company doesn't have to worry about paying off the mortgage. Cash flow should be strong enough to fund both dividends and the investment necessary to keep the company growing and lively. Earnings should progress on a steady uptrend—earnings growth need not be fabulous, but it should be at least *as great as the dividend growth that you expect*. In other words, for our purposes **annual earnings growth should be consistent, and it should be in the 5%–10% range, at a minimum.** Don't forget that dividends are paid from earnings, so you should be sure that dividends are a modest percentage of earnings (this is known as the payout ratio, earnings divided by dividends). The **payout ratio should be less than 60%** for nearly all stocks except qualifying utilities, publicly traded partnerships, and Real Estate Investment Trusts. Since dividends are paid from earnings, you want to be sure that earnings are large enough for a company to afford to pay the dividend, and large enough for the company to greater dividends next year and the years after. The lower the payout ratio the better.

Creditworthiness: a shortcut. Uh-oh, you might be thinking, "Am I going to have to learn to read a balance sheet and income statement?" Or, if you already know how, "am I going to have to spend my weekends going over quarterly reports to come up with my winners?" It might be fun to put on a pair of professorial glasses and scold you, like John Houseman in that "we do it the old-fashioned way" advertisement, tell you that if you really want to succeed as an investor you've got to do all the hard and puritanical work that the Lord requires. But the truth is, there's a shortcut to determining creditworthiness. And it's a good thing, too, because each kind of business has its own twists and tricks, and you really have to become a CPA or CFA to understand them all.

But we can afford to be a trifle naïve or passive, and let the experts—the established rating agencies—do the work for us. In all markets lenders and investors want to have a standard of evaluation for making large investment decisions, and rating agencies like Standard and Poor's and Moody's have made a big business out of maintaining an army of trained analysts who are able to evaluate all the different kinds of businesses and place them on a rating scale of creditworthiness. In effect, every company is rated on how risky it would be to buy their bonds, compared to, say, buying the bonds of the US Government (a bond buyer is actually a lender, of course). There are also financial ratings for stocks, published by Standard and Poor's and Value Line, among others—all of which can save you grubbily combing about in a company's financial statements.

To be sure, we've seen in the past five years that such "statements" can be deceptive, and a number of notable corporate frauds hid behind obfuscated statements to forward their schemes. But it does seem that the Sarbanes-Oxley laws have put a stop to mendacious company reporting.

Have the ratings agencies ever been wrong? It *has* happened—especially in those same cases of fraud (but then, the agencies were working, unbeknownst to them, with inaccurate numbers from the companies)—but they're mostly right. And the really short answer is this: could you do a better job across the broad market? It's entirely possible that when you get to know a specific company intimately you may come to understand that certain factors— like its market dominance or its revered brand names or great team of engineers—might be worth more in the real world than the accountants and auditors are giving it credit for, but those exceptions are hardly worth denying the great (and often free!) assistance you can receive from following the rating agency guides. This world is uncertain, and the future is even more uncertain. Given the level of uncertainty, S&P, Moody's, and Value Line should be viewed as "good enough," and certainly helpful.

Again, there's no point in going up to the borderline of financial quality, no point in stretching the boundaries so that a particular pet name can fit in the cut. We'll use only the highest rated segment of the corporate world. For our purposes, in the Standard and Poor's ranking system, a stock must have a **minimum credit rating of BBB+** to qualify. Among bond mavens, that's known as "investment grade," and we'd rather be on the next step up in the "A" range. (See Appendix C for information sources.) In my experience the Value Line Survey does a good job of rating the financial strength of equities (which are legally riskier than bonds, though bonds can be just as risky in the sense of being just as volatile in price) and here, too, the information is easily available at any library. In the Value Line stock ranking system, **a stock should rank B+ or better** for financial strength, and, as always, higher is better.

These rankings are quick and easy ways to avoid companies that might be potential booby traps from a financial standpoint, and the ratings probably have a lot more informational value than anything you could do yourself. The deal, over all, is a good one. But be aware that the dividend payout ratio isn't necessarily a factor in the credit ratings, since dividends are a discretionary or unfixed expense, so you'll always have to check that the ratio is less than 60% (except utilities and REITs as noted later on). Earnings should be at least 1.5 times the dividend.

Bear in mind also that the greatest credit rating in the world is not going to impress us unless the company is also a dividend-increaser.

Management Quality

High quality is not just financial. Any experienced investor knows that what you're really buying when you buy into a stock is the quality of management. Just as if you start a small business with a friend or spouse, or buy into one, you're really buying into the ability, honesty, integrity, and vision, of your partners. And you're buying into the viability of the business plan and business philosophy as well as its execution.

This component of quality doesn't show up as a neat number in the annual report—though a company with impeccable financials is likely to have good management, since great financial condition doesn't happen all by itself or by accident. Still, in looking at the management issue you have to lift your eyes up from your desk and take a good, long, panoramic look at what's before you.

Assuming you're not actually going to have lunch with the CEO (which might not get you the kind of information you want anyway), and realizing that the concept of "good management" is qualitative rather than an item that boils down to a simple number like book value (though "good management" is, in the end, the force behind all the straightforward quantitative numbers) there's a kind of checklist you can use to develop ideas about the quality of management.

Integrity. Does management ever lie? It's amazing how many managements, up against the wall and desperate, no doubt, will mislead analysts and the press about their prospects or the competitive position of their products. Often when promises or suggestive comments prove deceptive these stocks crash, making them sometimes seem like "bargains." Unless management is replaced, keep away. If you ever learn of a company that has publicly misled investors, or failed to reveal information that it should have, or is cited for improper or "aggressive" accounting practices, just cross it off your list. A funny odor in the basement might well be the first hint of corpses buried there.

Bear in mind that seasoned companies with high financial strength will rarely appear in this category, but you never know when things have changed or a new person tips what had been a balance of restraint into mendacity and avarice. The important point is that you don't have to be a shareholder in any company where values are questionable, and that includes companies with "lucky" insiders who manage to sell portions of their own shares just before bad news precipitates a stock decline.

Performance. How has the company performed in difficult times? This is the most important measure for you as an investor, for the real hidden agenda of all investors is to find a way to have a high confidence level when economic times are troublesome. Look back at periods of recession. Did earnings hold up? If the company is involved in a commodity like oil, examine how the company did during the long slide in oil prices during the 1980s. If a financial company, how is it affected by sharply rising interest rates. Past is not always prologue, but past performance in difficult times can at least give you some rational indication about how well a company will do in the next difficult period — which is sure to arrive sooner or later.

Too, you'll encounter a number of companies that seem to thrive during and just after weak periods in the economy or in their industry. These are sometimes countercyclical companies (a temporary-help agency would be an example), but often they're the jewels you seek. They're the companies that get even more aggressive to gain market share when their competitors are hiding in the trenches. They're the companies that make acquisitions when the acquiree is weak, the companies that buy up good talent when the market is loose, the companies that refinance their debt when rates have come down due to recession. Periods of weakness give well-managed companies an opportunity to expand—as opposed to companies that go chasing acquisitions merely because their own stock price is high.

Acquisitions. How well does the company absorb and integrate acquisitions? To my mind, this is one of the truest marks of outstanding management. First of all, it is a mark of good management to make acquisitions that *can* be easily absorbed and integrated. The choice of the target and the price paid are key factors, as well as the culture of the target and its distribution channels.

But even when an acquisition is well-considered in the first instance, it still represents a great test of management to bring together possibly disparate corporate cultures, to integrate information, manufacturing, and distribution systems, to rationalize product lines, to keep the good people that came with the deal and trim the dead wood. It's a daunting task, an entrepreneurial task, and companies that have shown an ability to complete this process successfully and quickly are managements that have shown they can use at least this one approach to growth. Not incidentally, they are also managements who've shown that you need not fear for the stability of the machine should they wish to attempt yet another acquisition. Indeed, since acquiring companies often sell off temporarily in the stock market due to secular arbitrage dealings, a proven acquirer makes a great buy should it decline on news of a new acquisition.

But beware of the mega-deal, the "transformative" acquisition. The largest deals have the worst record of success for shareholders, and even when they do work it frequently takes years for the synergies or cost savings envisioned to gain traction.

Brand Extension. Good managements tend to find ways to extend their brands, their services, their franchise, their strengths. You start out with a product as mundane as baking soda, and before you know it you've got a major new brand of toothpaste. You go from Oatmeal to Cheerios, from bank checking accounts to credit cards, from cars (in the case of Chrysler) to Jeeps and minivans, from chips to whole computers. M&M Mars may not have come up with a hundred ways to capitalize on the M&M brand, but they did come up with M&M Peanut. Don't laugh. There are an amazing number of companies—many of whom are long since dead—which have never learned to extrapolate from what they have, or at least have never learned to extrapolate successfully, have never learned to come up with the peanut, so to speak.

Franchise. Every company worth investing in has some kind of a <u>franchise or niche</u>. It may not be national, it may be as local as the reputation for honesty and fair dealing of a three-branch small-town bank. But that little bank is much more likely to be the kind of item we want in our compounding machine than a regional grocery chain which competes against three other regional grocery chains as well as five national grocery chains and has little to differentiate it from the others apart from the fact that they do not share the exact same address on the boulevard.

Quality Business. <u>The nature of the business itself</u> should be good quality, in a market capable of delivering moderate and consistent growth. Avoid fads and "new" goods or services like the plague. Sure, you'll miss a hot number or two, but new isn't what you want in a Single Best Investment. As we'll discuss later, the market for a company's products should be classical, it should be the necessities of life or important industrial niches. You want a company that can deliver <u>long-term consistent moderate growth, long-term dividend yields, long-term growth of yield</u>. These characteristics aren't apparent in either new companies or companies that are relying on new goods and services. Beware of pyramid marketing or network marketing companies (like Excel), or companies that are only marketers or resellers and have no real assets or products of their own. It sounds like a father's advice in an old movie: focus on real companies that make real things (or services) that real people need. The sleazier the basic underlying business, the more likely is the investor to wind up slimed.

High Current Yield

One might think that this part of the equation for picking an SBI stock is a no-brainer. However, current dividends have to be weighed against dividend growth to have real meaning. As we'll see, low current yield with high growth doesn't serve the SBI strategy, nor does a stock with a very high current yield but little or no growth.

There are lots of companies with good dividend growth, but if the current yield is too low at inception the investment meaning of that dividend growth is muted, if not lost. Rousing dividend growth in a low-yielding stock still probably serves the important purpose of signaling management's faith in the company's future prospects, but it doesn't do much for the net results of our compounding machine — at least not in only one lifetime.

Let's say you have a Single Best Investment pick that yields 4% today and shows a projected growth of yield at 10%. Compare that to a growth company with a 1% current yield and projected growth of yield at 20%. In three and a half years, the second stock will have a yield on original investment of 2%. In seven years, it will be 4%, in a little more than ten years it will be 8%. But our SBI turtle, with income growing at half the rate, will be at 8% in seven years, and 12% in about ten years.

If that rabbit can continue to post 20% dividend growth it will, indeed, catch up to and surpass our trusty tortoise, but there's a catch. Fast dividend growth (and 20% dividend growth is rare, indeed) is typically associated with fast growing stocks. In the heyday of the drug stocks, for example, you might have seen 20% dividend growth. But as the stocks get larger and more mature, their growth slows, and with that slowing, the dividend growth bogs down as well.

It's better to take a bird in the hand (oh, all right, one or two low-yielders in a portfolio if they're really standout and solid companies with long histories). The first goal for a compounding program ought to be to reach the average annualized return expectable from stock market investing—about 10% per year—from income alone as quickly as possible. You'll get there much more quickly if you start from a higher base level of income than if you only seek the maximum income growth each year. And, most important of all, if you use mature, financially secure, reliable companies, you'll insure that you actually get to your goal. Business is tough. There are a million ways for a company to lose its edge, to lose its way. As investors trying to create a compounding machine, we want to stay with proven winners, with companies that have been around the track a few times and know how to do their job consistently.

What should your base level of income be when implementing a Single Best Investment strategy? Unfortunately, we live in a relative world, so it all depends upon current market conditions. Obviously, the higher your starting yield the more quickly you'll get to your first compounding goal—but often the very highest yielding stocks don't offer enough growth of yield to grow your income up to the standards of a smoothly running compounding machine. Indeed, frequently the highest yielding stocks sell at high yields because there are palpable risks involved. In a way, the essence of what we're about in this strategy is *uncovering the high yielding stocks that aren't risky.* So there's always a balance to be drawn between high current income and projected growth of income.

At the moment the Standard and Poor's 500 Index offers a current yield (for the average stock) of about 1.7%—historically very low, but that's the hand an investor is dealt in 2005. The twenty-year treasury bond offers a yield of 4.60%, and the one-year treasury bill is priced to yield 2.5%. It's not

THE SINGLE BEST INVESTMENT STRATEGY APPLIED

too hard to obtain a current yield of 4% — over twice the level of the stock market. And as you've already seen from our compounding numbers, that's a decent starting place (1½ times the average is our minimum) if we can also obtain a growth of yield of 5% or better, which is also possible right now. At other moments in history or in the future you might find your starting yield can be as high as 6% for quality equities. But it's unlikely to be much lower than it is today, as we sit on what may very well be the tail end of a nearly twenty-year unwinding of inflation. In any event, at this moment in time a 4% yield is a reasonable portfolio target for initial income, using stocks that also manifest clear ability to continue steady and moderate growth into the future.

In the years to come, my guess is that you'll find yourself able to construct portfolios with somewhat higher current yields — now that dividends have once again become a priority for investors and the companies that provide them. In our firm we offer a portfolio with a current yield of over 5.5% (substantially better than long-term bonds!) that still offers 4% growth of yield and appreciation potential. In fact, it has consistently outperformed the S&P 500 since inception in 1998.

High Growth of Yield

How high should dividend growth be? How do you know what it will be? How can you project yield-growth?

First of all, you want growth of yield to be as high as you can get it. Bear in mind that very high recent growth of yield in a company doesn't necessarily imply future growth of yield at the same level. Often a company has implemented a dividend or dividend growth policy in only the past, say, five years, and is boosting the dividend fast in order to get up to a certain level, at which point the increases will slow. Many utilities have cut or omitted their dividends in recent years to deal with specific problems, and when the dividend is re-instituted it appears to be a huge grower — but that growth will level off as the yield approaches industry standards. In order to project dividend growth you've got to extrapolate into the future, but don't extrapolate too much, or based on the wrong factors.

You can look to the past if your subject is a mature company, since dividends are typically a matter of corporate policy. If a company has been increasing at a 10% annual rate, all other things being equal that rate will probably continue. But check to see what that 10% annual rate is made of. If year 5 showed a 15% increase, and year 4 a 12% increase, and year 3 a 10% increase, and year 2 an 8% increase, and year 1 a 6% increase, you're clearly not looking at an historic 10% grower. The rate should be stable or rising over the past five years. (See Appendix C for information sources.)

In general, you want to see a dividend growth rate that is at least higher than inflation, and with a margin of safety. So a minimum growth rate for dividends should be about 4% (utilities and others with a higher current yield might be a tad less). But, understanding the dynamics of an equity compounding machine built on high current yield enhanced by high growth of yield, you should really aim for a 10% growth of yield on your portfolio. If you can get that, your yield will double about every seven years, and so, according to our model, should the price of your stocks.

There are a few ways to project growth of yield. The easiest is to rely on the research of others. You'll find dividend-growth projections in Value Line, and many brokerage research reports will also deal with this issue (though you'll also find that many research analysts simply pay no attention to this key variable). Standard and Poor's also does a good job of tracking and projecting the growth of dividends. You can also call the company's investor relations department and ask them if there is a dividend growth policy. Failing that, ask about the dividend policy generally.

Many companies have, for example, a policy of paying out a certain percentage of their earnings in dividends. Once again, if you're dealing with a company that has a historic consistent rate of earnings growth, you can infer a dividend growth rate from the earnings growth rate. For example, if a stock pays 30% of its earnings out in dividends, and the earnings have grown and are projected to grow at about 10% per year, you can expect the dividends to grow a like amount (i.e., 30% of $1.00 is $.30, 30% of $1.10 is $.33). This is the method of projection that is most amply supported by available information: you can get the dividend policy from the company, and earnings growth projections are available on virtually every database as well as from brokerage reports.

As you can see, the need to establish a projection for dividend growth is the best argument for working with mature, reliable companies who've proven their mettle in the past and whose earnings going forward are going to be the most reliable. Many studies have shown that earnings prediction is an inexact science at best, but the prediction of growth stock, small stock, and newer company earnings is far more difficult than for established companies with experienced management and demonstrated success. In the end, though, the proof is in the pudding. You'll want to monitor your companies for dividend growth that meets your expectations, and a failure to grow the dividend or grow it at the appropriate rate will prove to be a key criteria for possible sale of the security. Don't forget, high yielding stocks have an investor constituency that wants dividend increases — management will continue a pattern of growth if at all possible — that's the arena in which they play.

Look also at the big picture to try to estimate if the growth you hope for is reasonable. While we try to avoid stocks that are "seriously" cyclical, there are times when a kind of cyclical event can impact an otherwise fine company positively or negatively and affect the dividend. If oil prices have been languishing, for example, a major integrated oil company may not feel comfortable boosting the dividend as much as in the past. Conversely, you may get dividend growth beyond expectations in an oil company if oil prices have risen sharply and the company is confident of buoyant markets for some years to come. Similar thinking would apply to broadly cyclical companies like autos, to interest-rate sensitives like banks, and to any company under a temporary cloud such as was the case with drug stocks at the start of the Clinton administration.

The strategy whose outlines we've been drawing for identifying Single Best Investment stocks does **not** require you to be a clever equity analyst. Stocks for projected high total returns merely have to fulfill the three parts of our formula: high quality + high current yield + high growth of yield. As Keats said of the Grecian Urn, that's all we know and all we need to know. The compounding machine that you create, driven slowly but inexorably higher by rising dividends, will bring you solid total returns over time.

Summing Up:

1. It's a simple formula: **High quality**
   + High _current_ yield
   + High _growth_ of yield
   = High total returns

2. High quality starts with high financial strength, and the ability and willingness to pay a rising dividend.
3. High quality includes management's honesty and management's ability to face challenges such as tough conditions or acquisitions, as well as to expand their niche.
4. High current dividend yield is always relative, but twice the current market average is a reasonable goal. 150% of the average is the minimum.
5. High growth of yield—income should rise at least as fast as inflation, the faster the better. Past may be prologue for dividend levels, but projected earnings growth must support projected dividend growth.

The "simple formula" is going to provide a group of candidates, most of which will prove to be reasonable holdings. In the next chapter we'll begin to look at some of the traditional tools investors have used to winnow out the biggest winners from the pool of contenders.

chapter 5

TRADITIONAL VALUATION TOOLS

Even once a varied buffet of SBI stocks is laid out before you, you'll find that the natural economic impulse is to seek for those items which you perceived to be cheap. At the same time, it's often difficult for the investing mind to accept the old maxim that "quality is always a bargain."

The quest for a stock that's "cheap" is a predictable activity of the human mind, since people do act to maximize their own self-interest whenever possible. But it's also a quest filled with tricks and traps, and is perhaps as important an element in ultimate investor failure as any single factor (other than the quest for the most glamorous stocks or the "latest thing"). We must respect the "efficiency" of the market. We need also to bear in mind that the quest for a "cheap" stock is, said differently, a quest to get something for nothing. Something for nothing, as we all know, can often be very expensive. When it comes to the world of business and economics we rarely knowingly **give** something for nothing. Why then should we expect it to be possible to **get** something for nothing?

However, many studies have shown that stocks that are lower-priced based on traditional valuation measures outperform more expensive stocks in the long term. As many scholars have pointed out (see Appendix A), investors appear to overpay for apparently superior growth prospects and underpay for assets. If investors overpay for growth, they have already discounted that growth in present prices. When growth slows or disappoints, stock prices are jolted out of their reveries. Over time, growth stocks tend to regress back to reality, while cheaper stocks tend to move higher on a relative basis, since much that unfolds in their stories tends to be viewed as a positive surprise.

In any event, once you've identified a "team" of good SBI candidates using the basic formula outlined in Chapter 4, you still need some tools to distinguish the best or most likely winners among those that make the initial cut. Buying *all* that qualify has actually proven to produce portfolios with outstanding returns and portfolio characteristics when studied quantitatively, but the size of such portfolios can be unwieldy for most investors. In Chapter 7 we'll review some technical analysis principles that may be of some help in timing your purchases, but there are a variety of fundamental factors that have been shown by scholars and practitioners to add value to stock portfolios. You should use these tools to reduce your field of candidates to a manageable number of stocks.

Price/Sales Ratio. Take price per share and divide by sales per share. For example, a company has $40 in sales per share, and the stock sells at $20. The price/sales ratio is .50. If it has $60 in sales, the ratio is 20/60, or .33. If it has $20 in sales, the ratio is 20/20, or 1.0. The idea here is that you are trying to establish value by determining how many dollars of sales you can get for one dollar of share price. O'Shaughnessy and others have found that this ratio is among the most useful of fundamental factors, a conclusion based on rigorous quantitative study (see *What Works On Wall Street*, McGraw-Hill, 1996). O'Shaughnessy tested factors such as price/sales against a large database from Standard & Poor's Compustat, going back to 1952. An investment in the fifty stocks with the lowest price/sales ratios nearly quadrupled the return from the entire universe under study, while an investment in the fifty stocks with the highest p/s ratios—the sort you see on high-flying growth stocks—was the worst performer of any factor studied, and underperformed T-bills. Risk-adjusted returns were higher for low price/sales stocks, and rolling period returns were consistently 30%–40% better than the entire universe.

Why is low price/sales a useful figure? The key concept here is that <u>revenues are the raw material of profit</u>. It's true that some businesses have high sales and low margins, always have and always will (grocery stores, for example), but <u>the very first prerequisite for a business is revenues</u>. If revenues are high relative to the stock prices, the business has an opportunity to show fast and sharp increases in profitability through cost controls and great efficiency/ productivity. Sharp increases in profitability will be met with the sharpest increases in stock price when the price is set by pessimistic buyers and sellers.

When a company's stock sells at a low price/sales ratio, the stock price in effect demonstrates investor pessimism about rising margins. When margins are improved even a bit, the effort goes straight to the bottom line, often surprising investors with the magnitude of earnings gains (earnings which are now available to pay dividend increases, of course!). So a low price/sales ratio is a very good thing, and it is even better if you can detect a trend of margin improvement (data arrays such as those in Value Line will display this trend). Companies with low price/sales ratios are prime targets for acquirers and other improvers of the breed, for obvious reasons. Once they get their house in order these companies can often show double-digit profit gains for a few years even without any sales growth! And once they have increased profitability, they can improve their marketing to increase sales, and on and on in the virtuous circle we all seek to find early on in the game.

According to O'Shaunessey, you should look for a price/sales ratio below 1.5. You should also modify this threshold depending on the industry you're looking at. In Appendix B we review various industry groups and appropriate modifications of the various valuation tools to account for the essential differences in different types of businesses.

Always check the industry norms. In technology you'll almost never find a stock priced with a price/sales ratio of 1.5, but then again you probably won't find a high yield stock either. In the oil industry, to take another example, you find that stocks are normally priced at below $3.00, so that the price/sales ratio you're looking for in a search for "value" should be under 2.25 times sales per share.

Price/Earnings Ratio. Divide the price per share by the earnings per share. If a stock sells at $50 and has $5 per share in annual earnings, the price/earnings ratio is 10. The price/earnings ratio, or P/E, is probably the most analyzed and studied factor among all the fundamental factors, and it is the one that most readily comes to hand when investors—whether professional or amateur—are seeking a quick handle on the expensiveness or cheapness of a stock. To my mind, what the P/E does is give you an idea of how quickly you'd get your money back if you owned the entire company, and the cash flow that wasn't represented by earnings was needed to run the business. Thus, in the example above, you'd get your money back in ten years if there was no earnings growth. To the extent that there is earnings growth, you'll get your money back sooner. That's why higher growth stocks normally have higher P/Es, even though the level of their growth, or even sometimes the fact of their growth, is often uncertain. It's also why interest rates affect stocks so strongly. The higher the interest rate, the more quickly I'll get my money back from bonds with little or no risk of ultimate loss. When the interest rate gets high enough, an investors sees, theoretically, that she'll get her money back so quickly from bonds that she doesn't want to take the risk of owning stocks.

The P/E ratios that investors "assign" to stocks derive from this "competition" with fixed income and are responsible for the bulk of equity price movements. The P/E is a proxy for investors' subjective mass opinion about the facts—one must assume that the facts are widely known by investors, and there's no reason they should not be—reflected as a price. How investors feel about a stock, taking into consideration all they know about it, become the price at which the stock sells. And, like price, the P/E is always changing—since the "P" in P/E changes all the time while the "E" is reported only once a quarter. At my firm we once did a study that showed that the average high-to-low price change for even the least volatile large-cap stocks was a minimum of 30% per year. The earnings for any given company only rarely change that much, so it must be the P/E!

There is a constant argument in the marketplace, obviously, over what the P/E for a given stock "should" be, and the P/E fluctuates as does the price. If a stock's P/E goes from 15 to 18, the P/E has been revalued upward by 20%, and the stock is 20% higher. If the stock also shows a 10% earnings increase, and that's reflected in the stock price in addition to the upward revaluation of the P/E ratio, the total return from the stock will be over 30%. If there's also a 5% dividend, that's over 35% total return. To put that in perspective, the market averages almost never gain 35% in a single year. But for investors to move a stock from a 15 P/E to a 20 P/E in a year is not really a great or uncommon feat, and it's likely to happen to any 15 P/E stock that comes in with a notable upside earnings surprise.

As you can see, P/E is a rather slippery concept, since a P/E is awarded by investors, not earned by the company. And it's dynamic, moving in lockstep with price except during quarterly earnings announcements, when there is a basis for the "E" to change. There's an optical illusion here: because P/E is the result of a division the whole numbers appear to move slowly. But if you look at P/E in decimal format, you'll see that it changes with the same volatility as price. Given that fact, can it really be useful as a guide to corporate fundamentals?

Probably not, in theory, but in practice P/E provides a very good marker for determining which stocks are in favor and which are out of favor—like pretty girls with many dates, stocks in favor get to sell at many times earnings more than the wallflowers. Too, it provides a good constant marker for dividing the high volatility stocks from the low volatility stocks—since as a general rule the lower P/E stocks are also the lower volatility stocks.

Interpreting P/Es

Most value experts use P/E as a guide to determining this shunned quality that holds within it the potential for reaping outsized profits when a company comes back into favor. Note that I'm not calling the stock "undervalued," merely out-of-favor. It may be priced low for good reason. Opportunities arise, however, when investors react to their own fears and sell a stock down to a low P/E when in fact its troubles are temporary or not even what they may have seemed when investors were busy selling. One thing is certain: it is a lot easier for a stock's P/E to go from 10 to 20 than for its earnings to double!

For us, the "valuation marker" use of P/E is fine, but we're really not smart enough to know in most cases if investor selling has been warranted. Mainly, one can use low P/E as a guide to low volatility. Why seek low volatility? That's really simple. Because we don't want high volatility in our portfolio. We want an investment that's easy to live with, a system that's easy to stick with, and high volatility, friends, is not part of that picture. If you want the rush of riding Iomega from 10 to 40 and then back to 10, do it with your "play" money, not with your investment program.

Unless a stock has had an "excusable" year of poor earnings recently, the minimum requirement for a Single Best Investment stock is that it have a P/E of less than the market. The P/E must be, at a minimum, less than the reciprocal of the long-term bond rate. That is, if the bond rate is 5%, the reciprocal (5% divided into 100%) is 20. The reciprocal of the bond rate is a fair P/E for the stock market when inflation is historically low or moderate—this has been true for decades past, and it's also based on the return-of-capital logic noted above. As I write, for example, the market P/E calculated on the past twelve month's earnings (for the average S&P 500 stock) is 24, but the bond rate is at 6%. That means my maximum P/E for a new buy will be less than 18—and it also means that the current market is expensive.

In fact, you'll find that P/Es on SBI stocks are normally much lower than the market as well as the "fair rate," since high-yielding stocks normally occupy the lower deciles of the P/E universe. But we need to establish a higher limit (i.e., the market P/E) in case you encounter, for example, a good growth industrial company with an intriguing story and want to add it. I generally believe in trying to work well below the limits that have been established, but there must be a limit somewhere, there must be a line drawn in the sand, else the mind will tend to rationalize what it wants to do and alter the standards in every different kind of market.

As was the case with price/sales ratios, P/Es should also be evaluated in the context of the industry group of which the particular stock is a member. Utilities and other traditionally slow-growth stocks will typically show low P/Es. The same is true for banks and insurance companies. Cyclical companies like auto makers, paper, and chemicals will show low P/Es when earnings have been high, and high P/Es when earnings have been low (investors are loathe to pay up for earnings at the top of a cycle, figuring that cyclicals have no place to go but down when times have already been very good). Technology stocks ordinarily sell at high P/Es, so when this ratio is low for them you'll usually find the stocks have been out of favor and may be good buys. More often than not, though, I've found that skepticism about a tech stock, as expressed in an apparent low P/E, is borne out by troubles that only come to light later. Here, as elsewhere, the notion of "bargains" is a tricky one. P/E measurement is a kind of ex post facto determination, and it's probably safe to say that in most cases the P/E is the right P/E under the circumstances.

What you want to find, of course, is a situation where the P/E reflects skepticism that's not really well founded, reflects fear of deterioration in a company that actually has the characteristics of one that can improve. Too, sometimes you can find a P/E that's out of line because the growth or momentum constituency has abandoned a stock with expected high growth—leaving stranded a stock that has evolved into a moderate growth item priced low relative to its real and uninflated prospects. As always, though, the prospects must "come true," and cheapness is only a quality that's affirmed in hindsight.

P/Es and "Undervalued" Stocks

The best way to determine if a low P/E stock is out of favor is to check its historical relative P/E. Rather than just looking at the absolute P/E, you'll get a better picture by looking at the P/E of the company relative to the market, and then relative to its own historic premium or discount to the market P/E. For example, if a company's P/E has historically been 125% of the market P/E and today it is 80% of the market P/E, there's a good chance that investors have soured on the stock to the point of irrationality, and that a fundamental recovery may generate oversized gains in the stock price. You can find relative P/E statistics in Value Line, among other places.

We've spent quite a bit of time on P/E because it's a tool so widely in use among stock analysts and in the press, it's a number you hear all the time. But in fact the various features we require of a stock almost guarantee a moderate P/E. Importantly, *the academic literature does not universally view P/E favorably as a decisive factor among successful stocks.* Indeed, many academics hold that there is no informational value at all in P/Es, though the studies that do find value invariably conclude that low-P/E stocks outperform high-P/E stocks over the long term. This might be seen as merely another way of saying that financials and utilities are good sectors for long term investors, but this conclusion applies to industrial, nonfinancial stocks as well. Some newly published studies assert that during recent periods P/E was not an important factor in determining pricing success for company stocks. But who knows, perhaps in the 1991–2010 period it will be the most powerful factor of all! The real lesson to take away from this, though, is that *many so-called experts will use analytic tools to come to a conclusion regarding the value of a stock despite the fact that the effectiveness of the tools is shown to be arguable.* No wonder stock prices jump around all the time!

Book Value

Theoretically, at least, book value is the rough market value of the company's assets. Without getting into all the details of depreciation adjustments and the like, book value, strictly speaking, is the value of all the company's measurable assets—buildings, factories, land, equipment, patents, copyrights, etc. I like to think of book value as the 5:00 a.m. value; what everything's worth before all the employees arrive and the machines start humming.

Book, like P/E, is another way of expressing valuation for a stock (though it doesn't tell you if a stock is cheap or dear, only the total picture of a company can tell you that). Stocks with lower valuations have historically outperformed the market, meaning that this factor is worth looking at—though hardly worth building a strategy around. In general, the closer a stock price to the company's book value per share the better (though, since we live in the real world which isn't always neat, there are certainly some exceptions. We'll discuss these later on).

Book value is another analytic tools of debatable merit, though there is certainly a rational basis for looking at it and there is a body of academic work supporting at least a moderate level of usefulness. We also need to be alert to adapt book value to the industry under scrutiny, and not just wantonly attempt to establish absolute parameters for all stocks. Too, if you can adjust book value with insight regarding the company's real-world circumstances, you might come up with a number that's in the range of a price that a private buyer would be willing to pay for the whole company—in which case you're at least halfway to being a true value investor.

It's definitely a relative measure. Today, the S&P 500 sells at nearly 6 times book value. I'm not that old (or so I tell myself), and I can remember when the S&P 500 sold at about book value—and not a farthing more! Clearly, if I'm a buyer of a company I'd like to buy assets at book value or less, since I'm more likely to get a good return on capital if I spend less capital. Lower is better when it comes to book value ratios (price per share divided by book value per share).

But you should never screen out stocks, or make "nice" distinctions between candidates, based on book value alone. The concept is too squirrely for that. There are simply all kinds of wonderful assets that never show up in book value. Let's say you built a great factory for making cola soda, and you produce a fabulous cola from that factory, which sells well throughout your marketing area. Your market price as a multiple of book value in the marketplace is going to depend upon what investors are willing to pay for your stock But your market-to-book is *never* going to be as great as Coca Cola.

Coke has a fabulous brand name, cultivated over decades by extensive spending and assiduous marketing and public relations. Where does the value of this brand name show up on the books? Nowhere, that's where. Nor, if you owned the best software company or investment bank, would the value of your excellent staff of professionals be reflected in book value. Nor, if you were an oil company, would the fact that many of your largest as yet unexplored oil leases are right next to the biggest oil find in history. The list goes on and on—there's much of intrinsic worth in a company, worth that a private buyer would pay for, that never shows up in the book value. This of course, makes book value a somewhat tentative concept insofar as it has value as an analytic tool.

On the other hand, as with P/E, there are extremes of high value and low value which do have at least some rough meaning, particularly as applied to an individual situation. A company selling at less than book value is selling at less than the value of its tangible assets. Whether it's a bargain or not even at that price remains to be seen from looking at the whole picture, but on its face such a company has got to be seen as selling at a "low" value. It's something like finding a used car whose price is below wholesale in Kelley's Blue Book. Of course you've got to be interested in a "discount" price, but you've also got to be wary about the possible _reasons_ for that discount price. If you discover that the only reason the bargain car is offered so cheaply is because it's been painted purple, you might have found a deal—assuming it doesn't cost too much to paint it beige. At the other end of the spectrum, many unseasoned concept stocks get pumped in the market and sell for 10 or 20 times book value. Here the stock is obviously selling on profound expectations about its future success—but you can be sure it's not selling on its investment merits as a business with a history and assets.

The Market/Book Ratio

The in-between realm of market-to-book is harder to pin down. (The ratio is found by dividing market price by book value). Most studies show that a low market/book valuation is a favorable factor, though how favorable is open to question. The best approach is to take a kind of real-estate attitude and look for comparables. Look to see what's normal in the industry in question. Look especially at any recent takeovers in the industry. These give you the best sense of all regarding what market/book "should" be, since there was at least one buyer willing to buy the whole caboodle at a given book/market. Again, though, be sure that a comparable really is a comparable. In general, we want the market/book ratio to be substantially lower than the average stock, and as close to book as possible. The closer you are to book value, the more "margin of safety," as Benjamin Graham put it, you have in case your overall investment thesis doesn't pan out. After all, there is surely more friction and it is surely more difficult for a stock to fall from book to half of book, than there is for a stock to fall from 10 times book to 5 times book. It's easy to hurt yourself if you fall off a ladder, harder to get hurt if you're already on the floor.

Temper your quest, though. It's probably not a good idea to obsess about getting *only* stocks with the lowest possible market/book prices, since that kind of cut will still bring you plenty of clinkers and exclude a universe of excellent possibilities. Book should, however, be lower than the market average. As of May 1998, to give you just one example of what's possible, my firm's portfolio shows an average market/book of 2.2. That's not rock-bottom, but it's less than 40% of the figure for the S&P 500, and our returns have been about 90% of the blue chips in what has been that latter's finest hour (three double-digit up years in a row).

Cash Flow and Cash Growth

All too often investors become enamored of the "names" in their portfolio, and forget that the real business of a company is to make money. Even in the highly evolved corporate culture of Hewlett Packard, a company much studied by business consultants, much emulated, and much honored with awards for visionary and exemplary management, the first tenet of their mission statement is that the purpose of the company is to "make a profit." That's what a company is, when all is said and done. It's a thing that makes a profit, or not. Just as a Single Best Investment stock is a thing that plays a part in an investor's compounding machine, or not. In both cases, if it's "not," then the thing will soon be gone.

As we know, there are many reasons to raise an eyebrow at reported profits, or earnings per share, since many factors that don't necessarily reveal the truth of the business can enter in to the earnings per share result. But what *must* be transparent is cash flow, and what must be *even more* transparent is growth of cash on hand.

Consider this: the corporation that best serves its investors will report the lowest earnings that it possibly can. Does that sound absurd, especially in view of Wall Street's obsession with quarterly earnings reports?

It might at first blush, but it will make a lot more sense if you remember that reported earnings are taxable (these are called pre-tax earnings). The more earnings a company reports, the more tax it pays. The more tax it pays, the less investors earn on their investment. However, the more earnings a company reports the better its stock will perform in the marketplace, so there's a kind of Catch-22 going on for which there's really no solution.

While lower reported earnings would be better for the company, most managements are richly rewarded with stock options, meaning that management has an interest that's different from a "private owner" of a business. On the other hand, stockholders, too, have an interest in seeing their share price go higher. The question, of course, is whether higher short-term stock price appreciation outweighs the long-term benefits of a company being able to husband its resources for long-term success. The answer is . . . we'll never know, because the system is in place and it has . . . momentum.

In any event, most *value* investors pay more attention to cash flow than to reported earnings. It's a better measure, because the nature of many businesses means that earnings may be relatively small compared to the overall cash generated, and not necessarily due to low margins.

For example, if the company has had a great deal of capital expense, earnings may appear unduly depressed, since earnings are reported after depreciation and amortization. So cash flow is a more transparent number than earnings, giving you a truer picture of how the basic business is doing. After all, the depreciation charges that reduce cash flow before the earnings number appears don't actually cost the company anything today; they're noncash charges. The company is actually "making" all the money it earns, but earnings appear lower due to the depreciation deductions.

Cash flow is notably important in determining the safety of dividends, since it shows you how much is actually available to pay them, though looking at earnings alone is safer, since that's a more conservative number—cash flow is always higher than earnings. However, in the occasional situation in which a dividend payout ratio may be on the high side, if you look to cash flow you may find there are ample resources to cover a dividend, though earnings might look skinny due to high depreciation. This is particularly true of REITs, with their notoriously high real estate depreciation.

O'Shaughnessy also provides the most recent testing of price/cash flow ratios as an investment variable. Results were similar to those with price/sales ratios, though not as strong. Low price/cash ratio stocks far outperformed their high ratio (high-priced) brethren. For reasons unknown, however, he found stocks with a low price/cash flow ratio to be rather more volatile than the average issue. However, here too the stocks with the highest ratios turned in a dismal showing. Clearly, investors buying stocks with high ratios of price to cash flow are expecting great things from the companies involved. Investors forget, business is a jungle. So much can go wrong. But, obviously, investors who pay high prices in the form of high key ratios are only considering what may go right.

Cash Growth

My favorite indicator of a healthy and secure mature company is wonderful, in my mind, because it's so simple and dumb. Even a kid with a lemonade stand can understand this one. *I want a company's cash and cash equivalents to be higher than last year at this time.* That means, in a manner of speaking, that it has more cash in the bank than it did last year (cash includes stocks, bonds, T-bills, etc.). How did it get that cash? Plain and simple: by taking in more than it spent.

This is almost as good a test of the true merits of a mature company as dividend growth! And, in fact, it is one of the elements you can use to ensure that dividend growth will be forthcoming.

There are plenty of perfectly good reasons why a company might not show up well on this measure: a capital expansion might be draining cash, or a restructuring, or an acquisition, or a huge marketing push. But there's only one reason why a company will show more cash this year than last (unless it has done a stock offering or sold a substantial asset)—it actually earned the money. In reality, as opposed to "on the books."

Not only does growth of cash tell you real things about a company's operations, it also gives you material for the dreams an investor dreams. Since we're looking only at dividend growth companies here, growth of cash certainly implies future dividend growth—for we know the company has cash on hand to increase the dividend. Cash that builds up often leads to a stock buy-back—which is the next best thing to a dividend increase, because it reduces the number of shares outstanding, thus raising earnings per share, and, once again, the cash per share that's available to pay dividends. Too, increased cash gives a company an opportunity to expand through acquisition, and it also makes the company more appealing as an acquisition target. Basically, cash growth is a measure of success, just as you feel more successful in your own life if you have more savings at the end of this year than you did at the end of last year. There are some good reasons why a company might not show cash growth, but whenever you see it, it's a major plus.

A Takeover

Speculating about which companies may get taken over is a reasonably good way to diminish your investment account and to develop frustration rashes. But when deciding between two Single Best Investment candidates, for example, the features that make a company takeover bait are also normally features which point to more attractive valuation. So this is another "litmus" test that can be used, as long as you don't go wild dreaming of deals that no one's thinking of doing or may ever do.

Lots of cash that's not put to use relatively quickly might single out a company as a takeover candidate. In our discussion about cash growth above, you may have wanted to take the phenomenon to its logical extreme, envisioning a pile of cash ever mounting, mounting, mounting, as the company's success brings more and better growth of cash each year. Obviously, this cannot go on in a never-ending cycle. Indeed, the more cash and current assets a company builds up, the better an investment it is, as Benjamin Graham pointed out, but not because it *has* the cash. What's important are the *implications* of having the cash. In other words, what might the company do with that money?

As mentioned, it can increase the dividend, it can buy back shares, it can reduce debt, it can buy another company or expand internally. But what if it does none of these things, or only does a little bit? Some managements just love to have a big wad under the mattress, or they're simply slow to act, slow to make decisions. Or they can't find just the right opportunity. In the meantime, along comes another company, or a financial acquirer, who says, "Gee, this stock is selling for $16 per share but it has $10 per share in cash or quickly realizable assets. If I pay $20 per share I'll get $10 back out of the till, so it's actually only gonna cost me $10. Not bad." This goes on all the time. Heavy cash is honey to a dealmaker, and dealmakers are scanning the world for situations where they can gain a "margin of safety" through buying an operating concern that also generates and possesses lots of cash. When stocks were much cheaper, in the 1970s and 1980s, corporate cash was exactly what the LBO specialists looked for. And when they found it they'd just go out and borrow the money to do the deal—since the cash would quickly pay down a good portion of the debt, and the "cash machine" being acquired would take care of the rest.

For an acquiring company, high cash and growth of cash is an attraction for the same reasons, but an acquirer is also trying to expand its own market share, or add complementary lines of business, or simply take out a competitor.

Strategic fits are also interesting to think about (again, consider these, but don't dream of instant riches. In a way, the consideration of a company's takeover potential is merely a way to focus yourself on the total picture of value, both quantitative and qualitative, a way to cast yourself in the role of a private buyer).

Let's say you're looking at a bank in New Jersey. Such a bank offers an obvious strategic fit for a northern bank like Citicorp wishing to expand south, or a southern bank like First Union or NationsBank trying to take over the northeast. Like a key chess piece, the New Jersey bank becomes worth more than it's "paper" value because of the way it fits into someone else's plans. And that extra value probably gets realized in the marketplace sooner than would otherwise be the case because there is a "natural" buyer out there in the wings. What if your name is Deutche Telecom? Wouldn't you like to expand in the US through buying a long distance company like Quest, just as British Telecom tried to buy MCI? If you manufacture artificial hands, don't you think it's about time you thought about buying a prosthetic wrist company?

Insiders

Insiders can give you insight into the merits of an investment. There are two aspects to consider: how much of an interest do insiders (management and board members) hold in the company's stock, and what have they been doing with their shares lately? "Insider" has some long and lengthy definitions from a legal point of view, but for our purposes insiders are board members and management.

There are many companies, including many of the largest, in which insiders own a very small percentage of the stock outstanding. Often, less than 5% of shares are held by insiders. This means that the company winds up being run for the benefit of managers rather than shareholders. While it's true that management typically benefits from increased share prices through incentive stock options, who wants to be a partner with someone who's got no "blood" money in the deal? You want management that's going to look to the long term, that's going to take calculated risks to enhance the company's future, that's neither going to remain static nor bet the farm on any one deal. As a true long-term investor, you want your partners to have the long-term health of the company from a shareholder perspective as their only perspective. Clearly, you'll favor companies where insiders own at least 15% of the stock, and the more the better.

Insiders often have proven to be quite "lucky" in timing the buys and sells of their own company stock (using, say, a one-year time horizon). While there's no reason to expect that a corporate insider has any better idea about what the overall market will do than anyone else, extraordinary activity among insiders on the buy or sell side is often associated with subsequent positive or negative company fundamental development. Bear in mind that there are lots of reasons for an insider to sell stock: to pay taxes on options exercised, to pay for a home purchase or schooling, to diversify his or her holdings, to invest in yet another of his father-in-law's crackpot schemes. However, there is also an old saying about the reasons for insider sales: "insiders never sell because they think the stock price is going higher." Rather than dwell on that aspect, though, I think one really ought to focus on unusual buying. The converse, of course, is that insiders never buy because they think the stock price is going down. While there are possible reasons to "excuse" selling by insiders, there can really only be one reason for insiders to buy stock (excluding stock-option related transactions) in their own company *at a particular point in time:* either it is under-appreciated, or good things not yet recognized by the market are happening. Focus on instances where multiple insiders buy together, or where an insider buys at a notable level, say a million dollars or more. It's hard to pin a number on this factor since each company insider pattern is different and you do need to parse out the incentive options transactions, but there are several services that specialize in insider activity that can give you some help. See Appendix C for further information on services that track insider activity.

A recent study by Lakonishok and Lee cast both some cold water and some warm water on the theory that insiders can point the way to profits. When they examined all stocks as a whole, they found that there was no real advantage to buying, for example, stocks that insiders had been buying and selling the ones insiders had been selling. However, they found an "anomaly": if companies are less than $300 million in capitalization, you can profitably follow insiders. SBI stocks tend to fall into higher capitalization levels—because they are mature companies—but there are certainly a portfolio's worth of items that fall under the $300 million mark, if you want to focus on this valuation "extra."

Summing Up:

The traditional valuation measures which can be helpful are:

1. Price/sales ratio below 1.5.
2. Price/earnings ratio less than the average and less than the reciprocal of the bond interest rate.
3. Price/book value lower than the market, the lower the better.
4. Seek cash greater this year than last year.
5. Takeover possibility—based on financials or strategic fit.
6. Insider activity—increased buying is more important than selling. More relevant to small stocks than large ones.

chapter 6

DOES UNDERVALUATION EXIST?
THE STORY OF THE STOCK

If there's one universal constant in the market, it's the claim of money managers and brokers that they seek only "undervalued" stocks. I've never heard a manager or broker proclaim that their favorite stocks were overvalued, or even fairly valued. There's certainly nothing wrong with seeking bargains and trying to follow the old maxim of "buying low," but all these claims seem to me disingenuous at best. Perhaps we're merely dealing with an insensitivity to language or an excessive use of jargon. But how all these would-be's whose portfolios consistently underperform the averages could claim to buy only undervalued stocks is beyond me.

The quest for so-called "undervalued" stocks is a tricky one, resting upon a questionable premise. What would lead an average individual investor to believe—for that matter what would lead a professional investor with a team of assistants to believe—that the investor can recognize an "undervalued" stock whereas all the rest of the world, all the trillions of dollars of brain and computing power, all the armies of researchers and global profit-seekers, cannot? When you think about it, the view that a particular stock is undervalued can only be seen as sheer arrogance. (Recall that one of the insights from Behavioral Finance is that investors consistently overestimate their abilities and prescience.)

It is as if these proselytizers were saying, "I'm smarter and more perceptive than all those other investors out there who are trying their hardest to make money in the market." Would that it were so! Such a genius would have all the money!

The fact is, if a stock were truly undervalued, with no question about it and no risk, buyers would be able to get something for nothing. Let's agree that the world doesn't work that way.

This notion that a stock is "undervalued" flies in the face of any notion of market efficiency, and it certainly flies in the face of the fact that today, more than ever before, all relevant information about a company is instantly available to any investor in the world via electronic communication. I've mentioned this before, but it's important enough to repeat. You're not alone with your information today. No investor is. All the information you can legally use is at your fingertips on the web, and in the numerous business publications and media which are pumping out the facts as fast their reporters can speak or pen the words. This is not just available to big-time fund managers. *No one knows more than anyone else* at this point, save company management.

The price of a stock today, then, depends upon investor opinion (do investors want these shares now, or are they apathetic?) of facts that have been exposed for all to see. If twelve brokerage firms cover a company, three may have "strong buy" ratings, three may have "neutral" ratings (only about 1.5% of stocks ever carry a "sell" ranking), and six may have ratings somewhere in between. The world of the actual market of buyers and sellers is the same. Investors come to different opinions based on the same set of facts, and the weight of their decisions is what determines the price of a stock (within some unspoken maximum and minimum boundary band which delimits the impossibly outrageous limits of pricing). The price of any stock today is, in effect, a quantified opinion, quantified as a number, a price.

"Undervaluation" is really, consciously or unconsciously, a code word. What's really meant is the **belief**:

1. That the company will do better in the future and investors will recognize this through a willingness to pay higher prices in the future for those still-to-come improvements, or
2. That investors are being overly emotional about a company's problems or changes, and over time investors will come to see the errors of their ways, come to see that the company has more power as a business than they'd given it credit for and are currently willing to pay for it.

But both these possible beliefs are only beliefs, the truth of which will only be known when times has passed. In either case the important view is that the company will do better, not worse, in the future, and the stock price will follow. (Even pure asset value investors don't get interested if they think a company is going to do worse and worse.) Well, that's not really analysis; it's more a kind of attitude, a kind of common sense. I use it myself. I say, "Companies that have done well in the past are likely to do well in the future. Let me try to buy them at a reasonable price, since no one's going to let me walk off with them on the cheap."

True, there are rare moments when investors toss away a perfectly good company for not-so-good reasons, but most of the time there aren't many if any real bargains available. Other investors are smart too: the true bargains get snapped up as quickly as they are found. Many years ago I worked in the real estate business in Manhattan. When I came across a naïve seller offering a property below market, do you think I offered this property to clients of the firm? Of course not! I arranged to buy it myself!

But the quest for undervaluation isn't the real quest for long-term investors. (Even a fairly-valued stock should be acceptable if it is going to deliver the kinds of dividend-growth performance we seek.) The price of a stock next year, and its price gains or losses, doesn't just depend on "under" or "over" valuation today. It also represents what has happened to the world and to the company in the space of time between today and next year. There's a kind of narrative involved, the real-life true adventures of a company as it progresses through time, its pratfalls and successes, its agony of defeat, its thrill of victory.

The inarticulate, hidden meaning of "undervalued" is that a stock has a proposed story, and the believer in undervaluation believes that the story will come true. As in the movies, there's not just one story. There are millions of stories, each one a little different, each with different characters and plot twists.

It might be a simple as: *I believe this stock will grow its earnings 10% next year, and in that case the stock will be 10% higher, plus I'll get my dividend.* Or it might be more complex: *this company is in the process of selling off a division that never earned them any money. They're going to show larger-than-expected profits, and they'll do a stock buy-back with the proceeds!* Or it might be the dream of a Great Tailwind: *oil prices are going to go through the roof next year; this drilling company will be the biggest beneficiary.*

Whatever the story, it's always about the future, and the future is always ultimately unknowable. There are only probabilities. And there are factors, influences. What will interest rates be a year from now? What will inflation be? Can this company's story come true if interest rates rise? If the dollar gets very weak? The factors proliferate, and the more they proliferate the more complex and variable the "story" becomes.

But every opinion about a stock is really an implicit story, a narrative about what will happen in the future. If Con Edison sold so many gigawatts of power in 1998, I believe they will sell at least that many in 1999. That's a story, a narrative about what will come to pass over the course of the next year. A likely story, a boring story, but every bit as much of a story as the story about the little biotech company that has a drug that prevents tumors from growing.

So to invest you must turn away from ideas of "undervaluation," since they are really mute notions, incomplete and inadequate expressions of the story of the stock. No stock is undervalued today, for today it is "worth" what investors are willing to pay for it, no more and no less. Will it be worth more tomorrow, a year from now, ten years from now? That depends on whether or not its story comes true. The real questions then, are only two: how likely is the story to come true? And how much is the stock likely to sell for if it does?

The Story of the Stock

You won't hear professional investors talking about this, nor has there been any academic study done, but I believe that in the end investors make their buying decisions more or less holistically, looking at the whole picture of a company, the whole story. Most investors screen, either overtly with software programs or unconsciously through their operative biases, for a general type of stock they're looking for. Then they add up the features of each, trying to discern the overall picture. It's not so different from buying a house—you might look at two dozen homes, tallying up the features of each and the problems of each, finding comparisons that are easy to make and finding comparisons that are hard to make because each house is different, holding pictures of each in your mind's eye, picturing yourself reading the Sunday paper over coffee in each, finally deciding on just that one single dreamhouse versus the others—for reasons you're not totally sure of. It's something about the whole deal . . . it *feels* right . . . .

With stocks, the situation is just a hair less emotional, and we can separate out for analysis some of the pieces that make up the whole picture. There is, of course, in a Single Best Investment stock, the triple requirement of high quality, high yield, and high projected growth of yield—something like requiring five bedrooms, five baths, and a good location in that perfect home. And there are value measures, most of which tend to fall into place if a company meets the triple formula, such as low price/sales, low P/E, low price/book, low price/cashflow, rising cash assets—the equivalents of eat-in kitchen, deluxe master bath, multiple fireplaces, pool, and cabana house.

But the "story" of the stock, the whole picture as it were, includes both the business position of a company in the world and the elements that *might* make it a much better company in the future than it is today. This latter might be due to an unfolding strategy of management, or it might just be that the company is tied to a major social or economic trend that happens to put it in the right place at the right time.

Look for a Stable Marketplace

Looking at the business position of the company—how it fits in the economy of the world, what its role is, what its environment is—we want to see first and foremost that the business of the company involves ***repeating sales***. The marketplace the company serves should be stable, proven, and it should need to pay the company for its product or service over and over again. Even better, the company should be involved in a product or service that's one of the necessities of life: food, shelter, comfort, economic survival, physical well-being, and, to a lesser extent, things that, if not necessities, are at least somewhat addictive (did you know that during the oil-country recession of the 1980s in Houston the number of cable subscribers continued to grow, while the number of telephone lines actually decreased?).

This means that the "normal" Single Best Investment stock is not, unless there is some special and unique value consideration, going to be the kind of company that makes washing machines or toys or swimming pools or hammers or sunglasses. It will not be a miner of copper or a producer of movies, not a dress manufacturer, not a lingerie catalog retailer, not a vacation home developer. It will definitely not be Kiwi Shoe Polish, which makes a product so fantastic that a little $2 can will last you for seven years! It will be companies with a predictable stream of cash flow that has been proven over the years, companies with reliable repeating sales, companies that do not hit a black hole when the economy goes soft or an upstart competitor attempts to grab some of the incumbent's turf. It will be companies with as little cyclicality as possible, companies you can own without being a prize-winning economist and knowing exactly where we are in the business cycle or which industries will be hot in the next 24 months. Companies where simple common sense can guide you regarding their probabilities for survival and prosperity.

Think of the best apartment house in the best part of town. Is it ever empty? Think of your liquor store or wine shop. Any bankruptcies locally in that business lately? Think of your local water or electric bill. Ever decide not to pay it?

When companies have reliable end-user demand for their products you don't wake up one day to find your company has lost a big contract and its stock is down 30%. Or that those robust sales everyone thought would develop over the quarter weren't so robust after all. Or that a big customer delayed taking delivery for a few months. All the surprises that can make investing a sour-stomach experience are warded off by stocks with reliable repeating sales. That's why these stocks are called "defensive." It's not that they don't do well in the market over long periods—indeed, they do as well as "offensive" stocks, and better on a risk-adjusted basis—it's that they defend you against ulcers and colitis.

But we'd also like to see something more than a fat old cash cow grazing in the fields and pumping out reliable milk every day at dusk. We'd like to see a growth kicker in the situation, a calf in the belly, as it were.

A Growth Kicker

Often the "kicker" is a division originally created to serve a company's own need which turns out to be a winner in the broad marketplace as it expands beyond intra-company services. GE Capital started out as a "floor plan" financing arm so that appliance dealers could display a large inventory of machines in their showrooms without having to pay cash up front for the inventory. The skills developed in this operation were readily transferable to financing retailers in other industries, and then, well why not, leasing airplanes, and hey, what about independent power plants, and on and on, until today GE Capital is a prime driver of General Electric's growth, and would be one of the largest companies in the world on a stand-alone basis. Smaller companies like ALLTEL found that the data processing division they needed to handle their billing and customer systems could also offer services to banks and many other companies, thereby giving them a "growth kicker" that would never have been possible in their main regulated local telephone business. Importantly, the growth kicker is built on a solid base of reliable cash flow from the parent, so it has the three things most new businesses lack: management skills, financial resources, and an important first customer—the parent.

So, in these cases, you'll want to look to the basic underlying cash flow of the primary business. Finding it acceptable, you'll look for circumstances where there is a standout subsidiary or division that can build extra growth in a controlled and evolutionary way on that solid base. *It not only has five bedrooms and five baths, but it also has a brand new sunroom, with a solar heated hot tub!*

Restructuring. There may also be a kicker in a kind of reverse form, when a company restructures to get rid of a money-losing or low-return subsidiary or division. This can have just as salutary an effect upon company performance and stock price appreciation as the more straightforward growth kicker noted above. Often a perfectly good company is being dragged down and held back by an earlier "diworsification," which, when sold or spun off, proves to have been an absolute albatross. Investors and Wall Street analysts are prompted to focus once again on the company's core business, and if they like what they find it's likely that valuations and growth estimates will rise shortly. If you think about it, there are really only two reasons why a company would voluntarily sell a piece of itself: to focus on its core business without distractions, or to dump a loser. Either way, restructurings have a way of receiving applause on Wall Street with a consistency that's never true of, for example, acquisitions.

Consolidation. On the other hand, great "consolidators," or companies that have been effective at making acquisitions in fragmented industries composed of many smaller competitors, have often achieved their "growth kicker" in this somewhat riskier fashion. There's more risk in growth-through-acquisition since the acquirer never totally and completely knows what it's buying, whether the price is right for an already existing entity, and whether the anticipated cost savings and blending of two different corporate cultures can actually be accomplished. Internal growth can be incremental and controlled; acquisition invites a host of problems. However, many companies have grown substantially by creating large enterprises from many small ones, to wit; WMX (formerly Waste Management), Blockbuster, and Trinity Industries are a few that come to mind. In recent years banks like NationsBank, Banc One, First Union, and others have been extremely successful "consolidating" the regional banking industry—a movement that's likely to have many more years left in it. Here both the acquirers and the acquirees have been great investments. If regular acquisition is the "growth kicker" that's part of the story of the stock you're looking at, be sure that it's not a new idea for the company. Be sure that the company has a proven record of success in such endeavors. If it does, you can count on the kicker, because in this large world there's always someone left to buy. If there isn't, the company's a monopoly and can raise prices without fear of competition.

Buybacks. Another "growth kicker" is a stock buyback. When a company buys back, say, 5% of its shares, earnings per share on the remaining shares instantly go up by five percent, as does their equity interest in the company's assets. Should the company also grow its earnings (which is quite likely if it has the wherewithal to buy back shares in the first place), the growth will be magnified by the share float reduction. Buybacks also show that management doesn't consider shareholders to be some sort of necessary evil, but as the parties-in-interest which they actually are, parties who deserve to share in the company's prosperity. There are a number of academic studies which support the value of share buybacks. Standard and Poor's did a recent study which made it clear, to me at least, that the magic number is 5%. A recent study by Prudential Securities quantitative analyst Melissa Brown also used the 5% benchmark, and found that large-cap companies with buyback programs outperformed large-caps as a whole, posting gains of 21% versus 15.5% for the total universe. Most other studies have found companies with buyback programs outperform their peers by 3-5% annually over long periods.

When you see a 5% buyback adopted by the board of directors, the stock should rise high on your list of buy candidates, since the statistical probabilities favor outperformance relative to other stocks for at least the next year. Too, managements that implement one buyback are highly likely to add to it or to enact another one as the first buyback comes to a close. On top of all the fundamental benefits, you've got a big buyer in the market for the stock, one who knows its details and prospects intimately, one who's more than happy to buy on dips and provide support—since the whole philosophy of a buyback is centered on increasing the share price over the long term. There are some analysts who are skeptical about the value of buybacks due to the fact that many are not completed. While one would have a difficult time premising a strategy entirely on buybacks, there's no doubt that a buyback is a definite "plus" when it appears as one of a constellation of features in the context of a stock which qualifies as a Single Best Investment candidate.

A Tailwind. Still another growth kicker occurs when a company happens to have raised its sails just where the wind is blowing. Remember the famous scene in *The Graduate* where Dustin Hoffman is advised that the key word in his future is "plastics"? The subtext, of course, is that even a passive young man can do well if he gets involved in a business with huge intrinsic growth. He'll be carried along on the wave, even if he's not as talented as all that. A company like AMP, the world leader in electrical connectors, might have remained a boring and unproductive story over the past twenty years had the world not become a giant entity of electrical connections. Corning Glass leveraged its expertise in all kinds of glass products to become the leader in glass fiber communications cable. American Water Works is able to add system after system across the country as municipalities find that they're unable or unwilling to make the capital improvements necessary to improve aging systems and systems that don't comply with new environmental regulations. Likewise, AES Corp. has been able to take advantage of the new wave of electricity deregulation to build and buy plants across the country, and it's also been able to find tremendous growth in supplying the world's developing countries with electric power. Without that mega-trend of newly developing nations, there would be no market for its services.

So the "story" of a stock includes more than buybacks and restructurings and management changes, it also includes the overall environment in which the company's functioning, the "wind" in which it's sailing. It would stray far from the principles of high quality, high yield, high growth of yield, if one were to merely become involved in "theme" investing. But macro factors shouldn't be ignored when comparing candidates to each other.

Bargains?

I've already made clear, I think, my view of the concept of undervaluation. A stock is always priced at its correct value today, for how can a stock have a value other than what investors are willing to buy and sell it for? But that statement does *include* situations where investors have become emotional about a stock, or even apathetic about a stock. The story of the stock, in effect, becomes the fact that, in the eyes of an investor, *other* investors are viewing the stock irrationally. Obviously, differing opinions are what makes a market, but in this case you must be convinced that there is palpable and extreme emotionalism attached to the price of the stock. One good case in which this appears with some regularity is when stocks perceived as growth items "miss their number"—come in with disappointing earnings. If the number's bad enough, growth investors dump the shares at any price, sometimes chopping 50% or more off a stock in a single day or week. Here we might find, in a particular situation, that while the stock has failed for now as a growth-stock vehicle, at current prices it might be a value prize. The emotionalism of individual investors and fund managers can create a temporary window of opportunity, when all the other factors are right.

But don't go using the "U" word. Just operate on the provisional hypothesis that the selling is excessive and due to secular factors in the market that will reverse rather than to the fundamentals of the company. Do you remember when the Three Mile Island nuclear reactor had a problem and had to shut down? Investors also shut down the holding company's stock, although General Public Utilities was a major mid-Atlantic utility with a long operating history and many other fine assets. The stock crashed like the market in 1929. And went on to become one of the best-performing investments in the world over the next ten years.

I will grant that from time to time special events and the special needs of certain fund managers as well as mass hysteria can create temporarily irrational pricings. But these are the rare exception, and you need to be quick and opportunistic to make use of them, because all the profit-hungry armies are always on the march, and they too know that temporary hysterics are usually healed fairly quickly if there is value in the company to support the healing.

In the normal course of events, there is no undervaluation, there are only stories which may or may not come true. For us, a good story means finding solid companies with good yields whose long-term prospects feature *moderate reliable growth,* growth which will be sufficient to boost the dividend, steadily increasing our current income and thereby creating upward pressure on the price of the stock. It's a boring story, but it works.

Summing Up:

1. Those who assert "undervaluation" are either arrogant or uncomprehending.
2. Information is everywhere; how could a stock be undervalued?
3. The idea of value is really an idea of narrative, of imagining what will happen in the future, in a story.
4. The story of the stock should include:
   a. Reliable and repeating sales with moderate increases.
   b. Some kind of growth kicker.

    c. Management that has shown concern for shareholder value through its actions (dividend increases, share buybacks).

    d. A real-world operating environment supportive of the notion that a company's past record of excellence won't be inhibited and will likely be enhanced in the future by visible economic trends.

5. Bargains may sometimes appear under special circumstances, but in general there are only stories with one degree or another of credibility.

6. The "normal" story is that the company has well defined long-term prospects, including the high probability of dividend increases which will eventually boost the value of the stock.

NOTE:

To say that a stock should have a comprehensible and credible story which we hope will unfold in the foreseeable future is very different from the idea of seeking a "story stock." This latter is a very different kind of beast. A "story stock" usually has some new technology or resource discovery, and sells at astronomical prices based on what might happen in the future. For us, the concept of a "story" is a set of characters and a plot line that supports the true investment appeal of a seasoned and solid business which can be evaluated using standard business ratios and models. In other words, the story alone is insufficient grounds for investment (whereas for "story stock" investors, a sexy story is the *sole* basis for the kind of commitment that can only be called speculation).

chapter 7

CHARTS CAN HELP YOU

This is a particularly interesting subject to me, since my management firm actually began life as an institutional research boutique specializing in proprietary quantitative technical analysis. In ordinary human-speak, during the early 1980s we taught a computer to read charts and to determine *which* of the signals and patterns that chart-readers use actually have investment value.

For years the university researchers had been holding up technical analysis—the evaluation of market action and only market action to determine if a stock is likely to perform well in the future on an absolute or relative basis—as a kind of laughing stock. It was an art practiced by fruits and flakes and nutcakes with no possible grounding in reality. A number of academicians undertook studies to show the valuelessness of technical analysis, though upon closer inspection one could see that these studies were merely an exercise undertaken to get published (and take another step toward tenure!), since no technical analyst of even intermediate skill would make use of the signals and patterns that the academics had "proven" to be of no value. It would be something like asserting that weather prediction is absolutely impossible in any time frame, and testing twenty students with wet index fingers in the air to prove this point.

Yet, ignored in these proofs was the Nobel prize winning work of Markowitz and Sharpe, which included the "mystery" of stocks with high "alpha"— high returns that could not be explained away merely on grounds that the stocks were more volatile, or that the market was volatile—which was basically the mystery of *relative performance.* Despite all the talk of market efficiency and roughly perfect pricing based on available information, certain stocks that exhibited high alpha for one year (high relative strength for one year) tended to outperform the market in the subsequent year. Since then numerous studies have confirmed the value of excess relative strength as an attractive feature of a stock. This confirmation in studies such as those by Jagadeesh and Titman, *Journal of Finance,* March 1993, and the esteemed Fama and French, *Journal of Finance,* March 1996, showing the statistical validity of relative strength as a factor, has of course been quickly hyped to excess in the creation of a "momentum style" of investing that has had extremely mixed results. But back when we got started with our research there was nothing but derision for the technical window on investing.

Fundamental Analysis Isn't the Last Word

I found the attitude hard to understand, since all investment strategies are ways of quantifying presumed or tested probabilities. The human mind, though, is in this case perhaps best typified by the mentality of the sports fan. Since the consensus view of the world assumes that stock prices are a consequence of corporate fundamental trends and not the other way around (and I'd never argue with that), it also assumes that any factor not directly connected to corporate fundamentals cannot possibly have any bearing on the price of a stock for any length of time. The conventional investment mind, locked into the primary (and not incorrect) assumption regarding cause and effect between fundamentals and prices, can only deal with stocks as if they were ballplayers.

This centerfielder has a great bat and a good arm, but that one has speed and outstanding defense. This one is old but might still have a few good seasons in him, that one is too young for the pressure. Comparing the *fundamental attributes* of stocks, or styles, or portfolios, and arguing about the relative merits of those possessing the attributes, or debating the attributes themselves, is all the professional world of investing can tolerate. If you come in and say "players and teams have hot streaks," you're going to be dismissed as raising issues that can't be discussed—since everyone knows that in the end the team that wins is the better team and the player with the most home runs is, by this causal conundrum, the best home run hitter.

Well, let me not get too far off on this tangent. Suffice it to say that practitioners and professionals at investing are uncomfortable with anything but the "story" of their strategy and the stocks that constitute it. All statements must connect to and be guided by the basic premise: the prices of stocks are a consequence of the company's fundamentals.

But this is really old-style economic thinking, the sort of thinking that's so married to the basic premise that it also assumes a perfect world in which the premise may operate. But we've already seen that Behavioral Finance has arisen as an entirely new field of economics which recognizes that investments live in a real world, not a perfect world, and investors are human beings who behave in all-too-human ways.

Since all the information about stocks is known to investors (now more than ever), there's little or no real explanation for the fact that prices change—though prices are changing all the time. It seems to me that if ideas that stocks are always "correctly" priced are going to hold water they have to somehow account for the fact that prices are changing all the time. Consider the "crash" of 1987. One day stocks were worth X, and the next day they were worth something like X minus 25%—although there was no fundamental news that would explain the difference. Clearly, the difference had something to do with the mechanics of futures trading and so-called portfolio insurance at the time, but the real difference in this and any other notable price change is that investor sentiment toward stocks had changed. Investor feelings are the most underrated factor in determining stock prices, certainly in determining short-term prices. But they are real and present at all times. When hard-line economists say that the price of a thing (or stock) is what buyers are willing to pay and what sellers are willing to sell for, they are simply agreeing with the notion that the subjective element in stock prices cannot be ignored.

Uncovering Investor Sentiment Through Technical Analysis

But how do you know how investors are feeling about the market or a particular stock? After all, the world is vast and the legions of investors just as vast, and you can't possibly interview even a fraction of them about their feelings. How do you know how investors are feeling?

The premise of technical analysis, the art and science of evaluating price charts, is that the subjective position of investors can be inferred from the manner in which investors are behaving, from the manner in which stocks are trading. This is not really too far out. If I see a couple laughing and hugging and holding hands, I can reasonably infer that they're loving each other. I could be wrong for some reason, or it might not last, but at that moment I feel some degree of confidence in identifying them as "in love" because they show all the signs of *"amore."*

While there is plenty of "noise" or trading that has no special meaning (perhaps most trading is noise), extraordinary trading reflected in price and volume patterns will, according to technical theory, enable you to predict performance—or at least performance relative to the average stock—for the future, and will lead to consequently extraordinary returns. By sifting through charts, or "maps" of prior price and volume history, technical analysts can find key *threshold points* which have signaled extended price movements in the past when breached, or outstanding *patterns of price and volume* which, likewise, have presaged important price moves. Like the gestures displayed by lovers that we may read as a sign, we also read price breakouts into new highs or breakdowns to new lows as a sign — of something about the company or the attitude of the investors who follow it. If a stock's normal high-to-low weekly price range is two points and it suddenly moves five points in a week, this abnormal behavior becomes worthy of note as a possible predictor of future price action.

But we know that there are many practitioners of technical analysis (each with his or her own spin on the matter), and we also know, to put it charitably, that not very many technical analysts are rich. Though these types often claim to have a crystal ball, let's just say that they don't have all the money yet. The question my partner and I set out to answer almost two decades ago was this: is there any merit in technical analysis, and, if so, where is it? In other words, which signals work?

Testing the Theories

One thing we knew for certain: stocks exhibit the characteristic of serial autocorrelation. Is that a fancy enough phrase? Autocorrelation — a thing is similar to itself. Serial — having the quality of existing in a series or repeating pattern. *Translation*: there are trends. Prices of individual stocks and the market clearly go in trends of three to eight months before reversing, we found, and individual stocks show similar patterns relative to the market average, over- or underperforming for three- to eight- months at a stretch. The question, of course, is when do those three- to eight- months periods begin, and when do they end?

We set up a computer database of over two thousand stocks, including about twenty years of price and volume data for each stock. We then proceeded to create algorithms to describe all the known technical patterns and signals that professional technicians have used throughout market history, writing formulas for everything from the most basic crossing of a moving average to Welles Wilder's RSI indicator, to several variations on stochastic (random) measurement. We also coded up most of my own original technical ideas, including such items as the Momentum-Gap Method, about which I had written a book in 1978. Partly on a hunch, we also created a rainbow of ways of looking at relative strength (the performance of a stock compared to the market average over a given period of time) and the many patterns of unfolding that relative strength can exhibit. This made sense to me. After all, the ideal in a portfolio would be to maintain a population of stocks that were all outperforming the average. And if we were right about serial auto-correlation, and if the Modern Portfolio Theorists were correct that "alpha" (another way of stating relative strength) persisted for more than one year, then it might be possible to identify, at any given point in time, a universe of stocks most likely to outperform on purely technical grounds.

Including all the algorithms and their variant cousins, each stock was passed through a screen of at least 300 formulas, and one day's worth of evaluating all the stocks amounted to several billion calculations.

What we found, more than four trillion calculations and many months of processing time later, was that when you tested the known technical approaches carefully by computer, requiring the computer to make buys and sells each and every time the requirements of a signal were fulfilled, there was very little that offered promise of outperforming the market—and we could find no strategy or signal which actually did outperform. To be fair, many if not most signals can't be coded in an absolute way, since there's much interpretation involved in the actual real-time use of these tools. Too, we found that where there was some added value or potential for it, the concentration of potency was in the large-capitalization stocks. Small stocks were apparently too easily moved by too few players, and false signals raged in the small company arena.

These conclusions were depressing. We'd spent a tremendous amount of time and energy, and had very little other than mountains of printouts to show for it. To be sure, we were willing to concede that no proof of technical efficacy was possible—at least not within the realm of our testing abilities. But we also undertook this project in the first place to find out what _worked_, not merely to discover all the things that didn't. And I was convinced that somewhere in our data we could find repeatable patterns that would generate excess returns . . . if only we could look at the data in the right way. The fact that stocks exhibited trends in both absolute and relative performance was as plain as the nose on my face. Why couldn't we come up with formulas that would identify the beginning and end of these trends?

We tried again, this time attempting to employ a principle that had become a staple in software development at IBM: information is more valuable when it is reinforced by the same conclusion emerging from different algorithms. With our usual penchant for grandiose jargon, we coined the phrase "multiple simultaneity" to describe the moment we were seeking, the moment in which multiple signals all come to the same conclusion and all arrive at the same time. Dr. Mike Howard, who had previously developed software for ballistic missile navigation systems, even created a graphic screen that looked like a Star Wars battlefield. When a signal was triggered, it sent a kind of ray gun across the screen to the point in the price chart where it was triggered. When many signals were triggered at once on the same price point, you could see it at a glance: light rays would converge on that spot from all directions—in all the colors and color gradations of the rainbow—and it would light up the screen like anti-aircraft fire over Baghdad.

We finally got some "good" answers, and by "good" I mean we finally got some of the kinds of answers we were looking for (and also realized that much of science must be biased by the quest to fulfilled a pre-empirical postulate or theory).

The Best Chart Patterns

I could easily fill a book with the conclusions we drew from our study quantifying the technical approach. To distill the issue for purposes of the strategy we're working with in this book, though, I'll propose that charts can help you with SBI investing, no matter what the Old Testament may claim to the contrary.

Charts help, but they're only one more tool: useful when employed as part of an array of analytic tools which include, primarily, fundamental factors affecting each individual stock. Charts can help you move more quickly if it's time to sell. Charts can help you wait for the prime buying moment if you're eyeing a candidate for your portfolio. As a timing device, charts can help you make decisions regarding adding to positions or lightening up. What charts can't do, all by themselves, is tell you what to buy and sell.

I've boiled down the useful information into a few useful precepts. I wouldn't suggest getting too involved in technical work—it will only confuse the issues and feed any latent obsessional tendencies you may have within your character.

The key item is not breakouts or moving average crossings or penetrations or support or resistance or cycles or any of the other terms technical analysts are wont to sling about. The key item is relative strength. Let me repeat that, for emphasis: **the key item is relative strength.**

Relative strength is, simply, how a stock has performed relative to the overall market (or any relevant index). It is calculated by dividing the price of a stock each day by the price of the index on that day. When companies are doing the right things and/or conditions in the market are right for them, investors tend to move in their direction, generating higher relative strength. Pay less attention to actual price change in a stock and more attention to relative strength. It is a better measure, for during times when most stocks are moving higher, looking only at price may give a deceptive impression of a stock's strength, when in fact it may merely be a proverbial boat that has been lifted by the tide. When stocks are declining, higher relative strength may be manifest in a lower rate of decline. But this is what you want: stocks that can weather declines without causing you to dump them out of fear.

There are all kinds of charts produced by various publishers as well as by computer software, that can display relative strength for you so you can see it at a glance (consult Appendix C for chart publishers and computer programs). Here I've reproduced a weekly chart of Clorox published by Securities Research in Boston, showing a rising stock with superior relative strength.

Note in Figure 7-1 the rising relative strength (A) of 1994 and again in 2001.

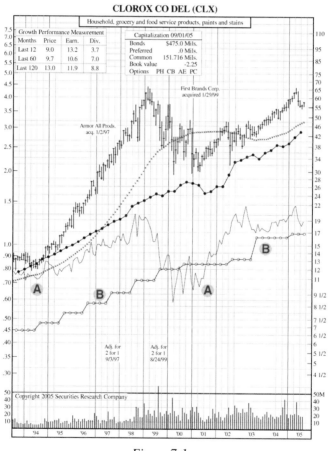

Figure 7-1

Note also the steady increases in dividends (B) from 1993 on forward, and the parallel relationship to earnings. Who would have thought such a stodgy old company would be worth three times as much in 1997 as it was in 1994, and twice as much in 2005 as in 2001. How could investors have been so dumb in 1994, or were they merely nearsighted?

In the next example (Figure 7-2), Procter and Gamble, one of the great repeating-business companies in the history of the world, comes tumbling down in 2000 on a relatively minor earnings miss. These are the moments that contrarian investors, value investors, and Single Best Investment investors cherish. But how do we know if we are looking at a blip or the bell ringing moment in which the past is forever lost in a future of clouds and fog? Look to the volume and relative strength.

Note the long-term progression in Figure 7-2 of earnings and dividend increases, with a relatively insignificant decline in 2000 (A). Volume on that decline was night and day compared to earlier trading (B), indicating a transfer of stock from weak hands to braver, stronger hands (remember, there is always a buyer on the other side of the trade). When relative strength began to rise in the months following, the technicals told us the coast was clear (C), and the nervous nellies would be cast into retrospective regret. Note that there was never a break in the steady march of dividend increases.

Six-Month Relative Weakness

One of the most intriguing things we found in our testing is that among the most powerful predictors for future price performance is at least *six months of relative weakness*, followed by a notable increase in relative strength. This is especially useful for our purposes, since as a stock goes down, its current yield, based on the dividend, increases. Buying stocks *after* a period of relative weakness has apparently ended gives you a

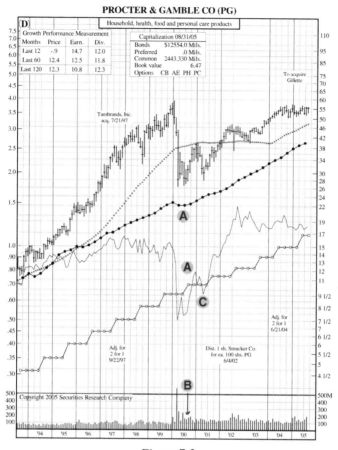

Figure 7-2

much higher probability of superior future performance. But what does "apparently ended" mean? There are a variety of patterns that can indicate the termination of relative weakness; the easiest and simplest for most investors to use is a conventional trend line break. A trend is first defined as a series (there's that word again!) of declining highs. It is broken when the most recent high is surpassed, as in the Praxair chart.

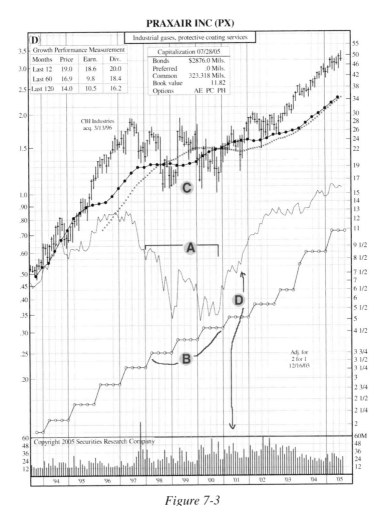

Figure 7-3

Praxair, a producer of industrial gases, showed miserable relative performance from 1997 through 2000 (A), despite the fact the dividends (B) and earnings (C) rose steadily through the period. This extreme disconnect between fundamentals and stock price would have proved frustrating indeed to any investor who didn't make use of a technical "road map," for it took four years until value emerged victorious. By using technicals as a guide, though, you could wait for relative strength to change course (D)—in this case accompanied by the plus factor of healthy relative volume (E). After all, who wants to hold a stock whose notable momentum characteristic is relative weakness when there are so many qualifying candidates exhibiting relative strength?

The prior period of relative weakness almost seems to be a time of pressure buildup for many stocks, and when the pressure's off they can substantially outperform. The weak period often represents a time of investor skepticism—much of PX's business is "old economy" and investors were generally cautious regarding the real, the rational, the time-tested, the necessary, during that period of the late nineties. But when skepticism turns to love it can be passionate and symphonic.

While the "formula" of requiring at least six months of underperformance coupled with a present indication of higher relative strength is the single most preferred pattern for buying the kind of stock we're after, reality is not always so neat that it will present you with ideal situations just when you're ready to invest.

When All Is in Concert

Bearing in mind that the fundamental formula of high quality, high current yield, and high growth of yield, is far more important than any technical pattern could ever be, and that technical "maps" are useful but not near as useful as a well-tuned analytic brain, the other type of pattern to look for when buying SBI stocks is one in which everything is in concert. Short term price trends should be moving higher, short term moving averages should be moving higher, longer-term prices trends should be rising, longer-term moving averages should be rising, and both short- and long-term relative strength should show an upward push. The trends should be mild, not sharp. They should look like the chart on the next page (Figure 7-4), implying an absence of sellers:

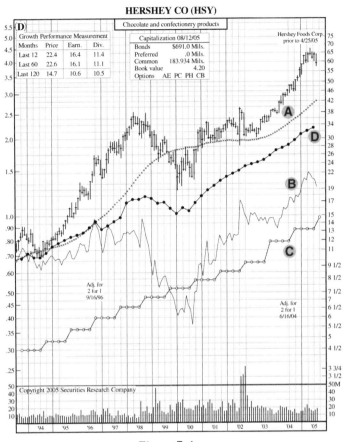

Figure 7-4

All of the key indicators for Hershey—short-term and long-term price (A) and relative strength (B) trends are on a modest and sustainable upward slope, and these technical factors support the fundamentals—dividends (C) and earnings in a steady climb (D).

There's no need to be a hero, and no need to go bottom fishing, especially if those kinds of stocks rattle your confidence. As has often been said, *quality is always a bargain.* Better to attach yourself to a quality company in mid-move than to fret over whether or not you paid the lowest price in the history of the world.

The trends should not look like this, showing an abundance of red-lipped and greedy buyers:

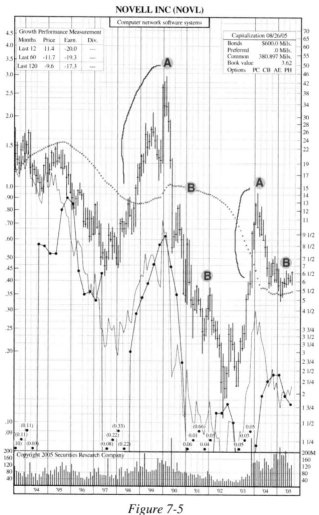

Figure 7-5

Once a stock has gone "parabolic" as at (A) you face all kinds of risk on the downside. It's actually <u>normal</u> for this kind of stock to offer short to intermediate term risk of 40%–50% (B). These are no fun to hold, even if the fundamentals are intact.

Do the two kinds of technical patterns to *favor* seem to contradict each other? The first, recall, seeks a stock that has been in a general long-term up trend (which is nearly always going to be the case with our high-quality universe) but has recently suffered from a relative price decline (for whatever reason) before beginning to show strength again. The second requires no prior decline at all. These are not contradictory; these are two patterns that have a positive statistical profile when scientifically tested over many years in many different kinds of markets. The first—requiring a prior period of underperformance—has much the higher "batting average" for successfully picking future winners, and its selections show less volatility. But if you are faced with a market that's been rising for a year, or a yearlong strong market for the kinds of stocks we buy, and you have money that needs to be invested, you won't find the ideal technical pattern, and you need a pattern that works under the conditions presented. In other words, there's more than one way to skin a cat, and you need to use the right sized knife for the job. Your parameters and techniques must always be in some sense adapted to current market conditions.

The Selling Climax

Here's another technical moment that we found to be of statistical value, and it's of particular interest to purchasers of Single Best Investment stocks. We found that volume of trading—a key ingredient in many a technician's arsenal of techniques—had almost no value in predicting future price change. But there was one key exception, and it is known as the "selling climax." Here we see an almost visual representation of panic.

A stock has been declining for some time, due either to a deterioration of company fundamentals or a reversion to the mean from previous overvaluation. It tends to go down in modest stair steps, as knowledgeable investors take each small rally as an opportunity to lighten their positions. For each step up the stock goes, it subsequently drops two steps down. Investors become increasingly nervous about the company's prospects, and, if not about its prospects, surely about its stock price. Slowly and inexorably the brokers begin to drop their earnings estimates, and then their ratings on the stock. The shares begin to exude a kind of odor, the odor of a loser. Then, one day, something bad happens. It might be a missed earnings report. It might be the loss of a contract. It might be a dry hole. It might be a big new product from a competitor. It might be the CEO jumps off a bridge. Whatever. Even though the stock has been declining and declining, on this day (or week, or month, depending on the time frame you're using), the bottom suddenly drops out. The stock may decline 20% or 40% or more. And the volume of trading is enormous. Every Chicken Little on Earth who's been holding these shares suddenly decides to dump them. The stock has its own private version of the 1987 crash. Under these conditions, stocks that might have traded a hundred thousand shares a day suddenly trade two million.

And that's the end of it. Like an earthquake, there can sometimes be minor aftershocks, but, nearly all the time, the volume climax marks a bottom. You need to watch a stock for a bit and not go diving into the turbulence to buy (there's usually ample time before it starts back up again); still, the selling climax marks the entrance of a stock onto your list of buy candidates. Where the stock fits our criteria on all other grounds—high quality, high current yield, high growth of yield—the selling climax indicates a draining of risk. And, since the yield increases for a stock as the price declines, selling climaxes often point out yield peaks in high-dividend-paying stocks.

Figure 7-6

There are always going to be scary moments for particular companies—lost clients, reporting errors, sudden changes of top management. The real issue, though, is whether or not these events have damaged the long-term value of a franchise. This leading international advertising agency became the object of investor fears in 2002, but there was nothing in the picture that would damage its long-term position. The selling climax (A) gave us an opportunity to enter a great stock cheaply. And guess what? Earnings and dividends continued to grow.

Figure 7-7

But often a major selling climax comes complete with a reason for investors to be scared. From 1999–2001, until the fall of Enron, many utilities attempted to grow to a level that the utility business simply could not realistically aspire to. They formed subsidiaries to create independent power generation, and took on debt outside the utility structure in quest of growth. In the case of XEL, they formed NRG to provide merchant generation. But the conservative managers of XEL, who had a wonderful long-term record of operating a solid utility, isolated the NRG debt so that XEL would not be liable. Investors didn't understand this—and there was always a possibility that a court would open up liability somehow — so when NRG encountered problems XEL was sold off massively. It's true they had to defer some dividend payments, but if you had faith in the company's ring-fencing of NRG debt, and you believed that the utility's monopoly franchise was valuable for the long term, you could have considered opening at least a speculative position in XEL (A). How often do you buy stocks that triple in two to three years?

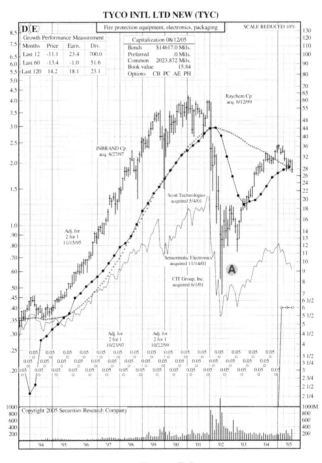

Figure 7-8

Tyco is a classic selling climax stock, where headlines and scandals obscure the business value of the company, its assets, and its ongoing operations. It's old news by now that Dennis Koslowski was using the company as a personal piggy bank to a criminal degree, but often forgotten in lurid articles about $5,000 shower curtains paid for with company money was the fact that he had built a prosperous conglomerate company that was dominant in its various markets. Investors smelled a rat and bailed, driving the company down from four times book value to about half book value. All the way down the company continued to pay the same dividends (stated as "irregular" but paid consistently every quarter), and bold investors betting on the business rather than just one set of managers, tripled and quadrupled positions bought when fear was highest (A).

To be sure, not every selling climax will have a happy ending. But the rewards are great enough to absorb some losers in the process. Certainly, when earnings and dividends are unharmed by whatever history is unfolding, SBI investors want to get very interested. Even when there are real troubles, however, selling climax stocks are worth a look if the company has had a long history and if it has a franchise of some kind, a business position difficult to re-create. If it was once an SBI with "all in concert," the question becomes: can it become so once again? Position yourself three or five years hence, looking back on today's events. Will they pass?

Look for the Turn

In general, with all of the patterns we've looked at (and the selling climax especially), technical analysis is most useful as a timing tool—and it is never more than a timing tool—in helping you to identify "the turn." Think of this as your little investing mantra for timing, "look for the turn." No matter how short or how long a time frame you are using when looking at charts, always try to buy when the price turns up. Remember, stocks exhibit the characteristic of "serial autocorrelation." They go in trends. When the trend has been against the stock, use technical analysis to see when it might have changed in favor of the stock. If you don't see a turn, don't buy. Many professions in this country are filled with former investors and traders who thought they were smart enough to pick the bottom. Whether you're looking for a long-term bottom or a short-term entry point, as the old saying goes, "let someone else's money make the bottom." This couldn't be more apt when dealing with SBI stocks. After all, you're going to be involved with each investment for a long, long, time. Why not be patient enough to wait for the best, or at least the better, moment to begin your relationship?

Technicals for Selling

Strictly speaking, one would think that a mirror image of the most promising buy patterns would be used for selling. If a rising relative strength after a period of relative underperformance is best for buying, then a falling relative strength after a period of relative outperformance is best for selling, right?

The answer is yes and no. Surely, looking only at the rationale of using technical patterns to gauge the attractiveness of a stock, you'd reverse your approach for selling. But there are two problems. First, the statistical profile of comparable signals for selling, as opposed to buying, is not a mirror image. The selling signals aren't nearly as accurate in terms of predicting direction or magnitude of a trend move.

Second, and more important, we *don't want to sell* these stocks, we're *not seeking to sell* these stocks. Whereas the technical picture may be helpful in delaying a buy decision on a candidate stock, or speeding up a decision to buy, once we're "in" we don't really own a stock any more—we own a part of a compounding machine.

We don't want to sell quickly, since we've taken a great deal of trouble to find a stock that can contribute to our compounding machine over a long period, and we certainly don't want to sell merely because the stock price has gotten the shakes in the short term on the tickertape.

Chapter 8 goes into some detail about how to hold an SBI stock, and when to sell. In general, technicals aren't useful for selling this kind of stock, because you want to hold it as long as possible, for a lifetime if you can. You want to let the compounding do its work over time. Once you're an owner, you're getting paid every quarter to wait out the rough patches, and you're getting paid more every year for doing so. Consider this: if you sell, you won't get paid anymore.

If you want to use technicals to help your buying, a few rules of thumb are all you need, and we'll review them in Chapter 10, "The Rules."

Summing Up:

1. Many reject technical analysis, but both academic and practical quantitative studies indicate it can be helpful.
2. The most important single factor is relative strength, the performance of an issue relative to a benchmark such as the market, or its industry group.
3. You should see short-term relative strength, but a prior period of relative weakness is not only acceptable, it is a plus.
4. Examine massive selling to determine if a "climax" has occurred.
5. Let there be a turn. Let the stock show at least some hints of good near-term performance before buying.
6. Technicals aren't so well adapted for selling, especially in the case of stocks that you intend to hold many years. Selling a stock based on a chart is hardly the same thing as choosing a stock from a list of qualifying candidates because its technicals cause the stock to stand out from the pack.

chapter 8

A GALLERY OF SINGLE BEST INVESTMENT STOCKS

In order to illustrate the Single Best Investment principles and selection techniques in action I'm displaying sample pages from the Value Line Investment Survey. Value Line isn't the only source of data or graphics regarding potential SBI candidates, but it's certainly a worthwhile source for the casual investor. Most of the companies included in the service are seasoned, the price of the service with weekly updates isn't prohibitive, and it's available at most libraries. The same information is available from other places such as Standard & Poor's and a variety of websites, but few alternatives can boast the concise historical display of 17 years of data that you'll find in Value Line. This is why I find it valuable; you can quickly spot long-term patterns and trends because the data is all laid out in front of you. Too, key ratios are shown in a sensible and logical manner, right where a user needs them.

For design reasons I've altered the look of the Value Line page a bit, showing less historical data though enough to satisfy our purposes. I've also eliminated the textual recommendations of the service: while

Value Line is more independent and generally more objective than, for example, brokerage house analysis, the SBI approach is *systematic* and no organization's evaluation is going to be consistent with the kinds of criteria we're looking for. In other words, a primary goal is to function without the influence of another party's criteria. So if you use the data from this or another service, try to ignore their evaluations. Some of my most successful stocks have had a low rating from the Value Line system, and other approaches that are heavily biased in favor of growth and momentum. Many SBI stocks are only average growers, but it is their consistency that makes for profits in the long run.

Please note: the following stocks are for illustration purposes only — to offer some detail regarding how to look for and how to analyze Single Best Investment stocks. While many might be stocks I'd want to consider today, the circumstances and valuation of a specific company are subject to change, and the lead time for a book is simply too long to permit concrete recommendations.

Read the discussion of the first stock carefully, as it includes extra information about how to read the data presentation on a Value Line page.

QUESTAR CORP (Figure 8-1) has been one of our best performing stocks, and we've used it in our firm's Utilities portfolio as well as our Income-Equity portfolio. To some extent we got lucky with this, as it benefited from mighty increases in the price of natural gas, but natural gas was "the story of the stock" for us, and when a stock has a clear growth kicker, you're going to get lucky sometimes. To follow the evaluation of this stock, start with the year 2000 column (A), where we were buyers (though it seemed everyone else in the world only wanted internet stocks at the time) in the mid to high teens.

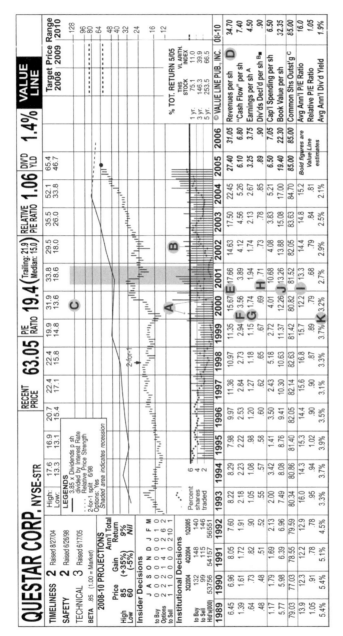

Figure 8-1

Looking upward from the year identifier you'll see the spiky vertical lines which indicate the monthly volume of trading in the stock (Value Line uses "percent of shares traded," which indicates the *percent* of all shares issued rather than the actual number of shares traded, but the *trends* in volume are the same whatever measure you use.) Within the volume note the dotted line, which shows the relative strength (B) of the stock—how it has performed compared to all the 1700 stocks in the Value Line universe. Above that, in the middle of the graph, are the range of high-to-low prices for each month, and the solid "value" line which represents the "normal" price-to-cash flow ratio, calculated by creating a "best fit" line based on past pricing and cash flow. At the top of the column (C) are the annual highs and lows, and various current valuation measures such as P/E ratio and current dividend yield.

Down below the year identifier you'll see some of the value measures that we've already discussed. The first line down, as indicated by the bold title all the way over on the right (D, under " Value Line Pub, Inc.") is the revenues per share—the number you would use to calculate a Price/Sales ratio. As you can see, in 2000 Questar had $15.67 in revenues per share (E), which is very close to the share price, giving us a Price/Sales ratio of about 1, two-thirds of our desired minimum of 1.5 for a P/S ratio, so the stock qualifies on that criteria. For a natural gas utility, which was the primary business of the company in 2000, a Price/Sales ratio of about 1 is fairly typical. Note that sales took a big jump in 2000—we'll get into that later, but you should always take note when revenues undergo a big change.

In the beginning of 2000 the stock also sold for a multiple of cash flow (the table line just below revenues) of about 5, also a reasonable number, and generally lower than the company's past history (F). Looking at earnings per share (G), we note that the prior two years had been a bit melancholy, although the company continued to raise dividends (H)—and, indeed, revenues and cash flow were merely flat. Particularly in the case of gas utilities, there is often an understandable period of slow earnings due to abnormal weather or regulatory lags, which can be forgiven in the right circumstances (which this company did offer).

At the time we purchased Questar it was selling at slightly-below average P/E (I) and book value multiple (J) for a gas utility, though it had reasonable growth in its service territory and fairly congenial regulation, with a yield of about 3.2% (K) and a good history of rising dividends. However, in looking more closely we saw that they had a small natural gas exploration and production subsidiary that had shown rising revenues and rising reserves for each of the prior five years. At the same time, there was talk in the gas industry that their exploration area, the Pinedale Anticline, might be—emphasize the "might"—one of the great new discoveries in North America. We saw that we could take no more risk than we would buying a normal regulated gas utility, but with considerable upside should they be sitting on a substantial field. Given their history of successful exploitation even without a major find, and given the fact that we clearly were not paying for any of this imagined upside potential, it seemed like a good choice for our portfolio.

So, we had a "story" for which we were not paying; the basic company without that story was a perfectly reasonable holding. The growth of natural gas in recent decades was known, and simply transporting it to users was a sound business with good prospects. This gave the company a kind of wind to its back whether or not its E&P division proved to be a long-term winner. We expected dividend increases from its basic business, and we hoped for more from its then-small and manageable but evolving subsidiary. Debt and equity were about equal, which is in the correct zone for a regulated utility, and their financial ratings were sound. The payout ratio was below 60%, also fine for a utility.

Things worked out even better than expected for Questar. Gas usage increased across the board, as virtually all new housing and all new electric generation used natural gas as the primary energy source. And, as time passed it became clearer and clearer that the Pinedale Anticline was indeed one of the big discoveries in North American gas. The little exploration subsidiary was sitting, to mix metaphors, on top of a gold mine. Further, as the overall economy expanded and economies in China, Eastern Europe, and India began to accelerate their own economic development, demand for gas reached almost stressful proportions, driving the price of natural gas higher than had ever been seen. So Questar benefited from both increased volumes and increased prices at the same time. The stock has risen over fourfold—rather muscular for a quiet little gas utility!

Note: At this point the company has been "discovered," and while ongoing potential remains great, it is now much more a gas producer than a utility, and much more vulnerable to changes in natural gas pricing. We've taken partial profits many times over the years, and expect to take more, but we're not adding shares at this point. While our income yield on original investment is a healthy 6% as I write, the current yield (the yield if you bought new shares today) is no longer large enough for a new purchase candidate.

EMERSON ELECTRIC (Figure 8-2). Emerson is the perfect picture of a steady moderate grower—even though at first blush it would seem to be involved in businesses that would be cyclical and sensitive to the ups and downs of the economy. The company manufactures a broad range of electrical products and systems, including electric motors of all kinds. Although this is not a repeating sales or "necessity" type of business, management obviously makes up for this with its ability to deliver increasing sales, earnings, and dividends through booms and recessions, slowdowns and speedups, strong dollars and weak, whatever. Look at the historical array. It just goes up and up and up, wherever you look. Clearly management of this "A" rated company knows how to succeed in their business. There were no big drops enabling buyers to scoop up a bargain in this one, but none were needed. Look at the dividend in 1991 (A). By 1998 it had about doubled (B) and the stock, helped by a roaring bull market, had

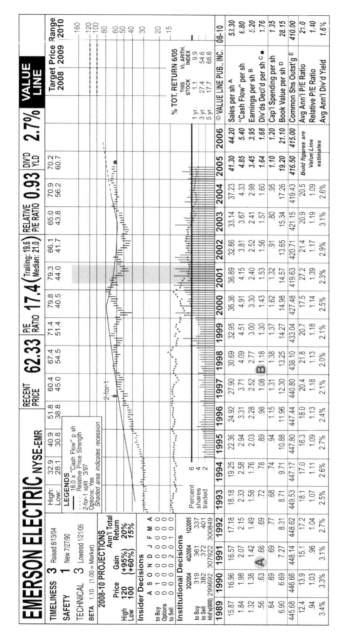

Figure 8-2

THE SINGLE BEST INVESTMENT

done a little better. What more can one say? If you hold a stock like EMR and the market gets scary, or the price softens up a bit, all you need to do is view the historic data array, roll over, and go back to sleep.

Emerson gives us a good view of the benefits of holding a solid, financially strong, well-managed company with a good (if perhaps not the highest) yield over the longer term. Through the tech bubble up and the bubble down, this company has remained a steady-eddie, with annual dividend increases averaging 8% a year. In 1995, with a P/E ratio in the mid-to-high teens and a dividend yield of close to 3%, it was not glaringly cheap or a "bargain." But it had among the longest of track records in providing steady earnings and dividend growth through strong and weak economies, rising and falling markets, with thousands and thousands of products addressing nearly every manufacturing segment.

Every annual number was rising for this company: revenues, cash flow, earnings, capital spending (needed to continue growth), book value, and dividends. Indeed, the power of compounding has become manifest here; from a current yield of just under 3% when purchased in 1995, over ten years the dividend has grown such that the income yield on original investment will be about 6% by the time you read this book. The question arises: would you like to own one of the handful of America's premier industrial companies for the long term, with a 6% yield? All you have to do is add it to your portfolio, and, most importantly, do nothing!

It is undoubtedly true that you would have had some gray days along the way, especially in 2001–2002, when having "electric" in your name was probably not helpful to your share price, but all the time you would be free to hold, knowing that you were being paid to wait by a solid and durable company. Persistent dividend increases were the only information you really needed in order to know that all was still well with the company, no matter what the market was doing. Not only did the dividend double during the overall ten-year period, but so did the stock price—and reinvesting dividends along the way would have increased the number of your shares by over 20%.

PITNEY BOWES (Figure 8-3). Often the stock's "story"—assuming all the "numbers" have lined up in order—has to do with the nature of its business, and, more than that, its "franchise." Noted investor Warren Buffett often appears to think that "franchise," the monopolistic characteristics that accrue from geographic advantage, or brand name, or industry dominance, is an investment variable which can almost determine the appeal of an investment all by itself. We need more, we need dividends and dividend growth to create our compounding machine, but a great "franchise" can be a thing of investment beauty—and it can definitely help ensure the durability of the machine.

Pitney Bowes, with its ubiquitous postage machines that are in daily usage in nearly every office of any size in America (plus many foreign countries), basically has its foot in the door, or its hand in the pocket, if you will, of every business of consequence in the land. What a customer list! And with little or no competition! The company has a gazillion opportunities to extend its brand name and sell more to the same group of customers, in addition to its virtual monopoly on postage meters and other mailing equipment.

Even so, if you look hard you can find a freckle or two on Pitney Bowes' record. In 1994 (A) and again in 2001(B), earnings were off a few pennies. Since those two years represent a recession and a slowdown, we can say that PBI has some exposure to the economic or business cycle. But it's very minor, nothing like, say, a steel or copper producer. Indeed, even in those two "bad" years cash flow still increased. And, more important, dividends increased as well, indicating management's view that short-term events such as a recession or economic slowdown are not really the keys to analyzing the company—even though investors may sell the shares off through myopic fear.

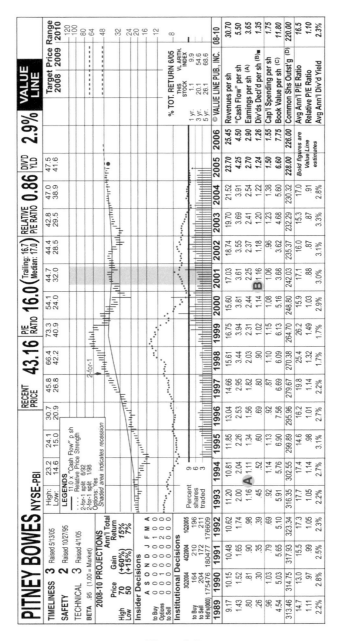

Figure 8-3

An investor who purchased this money-making machine in 1994, when investor confidence in America reached a temporary low ebb due to Fed interest rates hikes, might have had to stomach a decline until the end of 1994 (depending on the purchase timing), making this seem a sour move. But by reaffirming the decision through an examination of the company's past success in its "franchise" field, the investor would have been calm enough to hold on or buy more, and take advantage of the good run to come. Even after a large correction in 1999–2000 (partly on unfounded fears that internet companies would steal the company's franchise) when the dust settled, both dividends and stock price had more than doubled, and in the first half of that holding decade the stock was one of the best in the market. Current yield on shares purchased in 1994 would be over 6%, not including the benefits from dividend reinvestment.

AMSOUTH (Figure 8-4). Banks sometimes seem like a commodity type business, but they're not all the same. The "story" that may separate qualifying banks from others may be 1) exceptional and dynamic management, 2) a niche in the industry, 3) great demographics, or 4) like Questar, a successful evolving subsidiary. Amsouth, like many banks, was and is a financially strong company with a long history of rising dividends and earnings. I don't suppose its ATMs are that much different from anyone else's ATMs, but what highlights this one, as opposed to the mass of banks across the country, is the combination of good yield, yield growth, and great demographics in its Sunbelt territory.

After a mighty rally in the 1990s which brought the stock to an historically low yield, the company ran into some problems with its loan portfolio and reorganization, prompting its earnings to go flat in 1999 and 2000 and causing the stock to fall by half from what were somewhat overblown highs. What caught our eye, however, was management's 25% increase in dividends in 1999 and 15% increase in 2000 (A). While analysts up and down Wall Street were bemoaning a slowing of growth and profitability for the company, management was telling a rather different story about

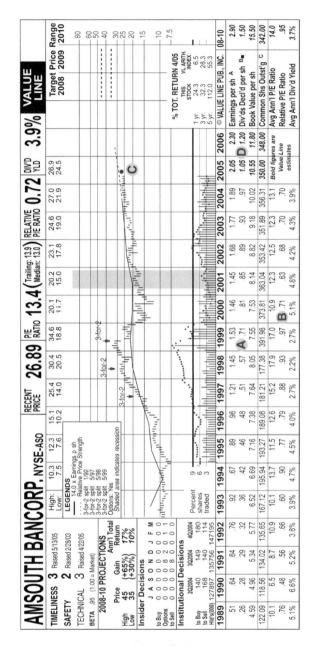

Figure 8-4

future prospects with its "vote" in favor of much higher dividend payouts. Investors should take note when a stock with the wind to its back—in the form of great demographics in the vibrant Sunbelt—makes substantial increases in dividends. By 2000 the stock was yielding over 5% and we found the turnaround prospects, for a company that had long since proved its ability to grow in a growing market, irresistible (B). As you can see, since 2000 the stock has nearly doubled (C), and, just as important, the dividend has continued to grow, reaching an 8% yield on original investment by 2005, soon to be a 10% yield on original investment (D). Of course earnings have recovered smartly, just as management had "predicted" with its major dividend increases. The P/E has risen only to 13.5 (E) from 10, the balance of the improvement in price being accomplished through rising earnings and commensurate rising dividends, which we expect to continue growing at near 10% for the foreseeable future.

JOHNSON & JOHNSON (Figure 8-5). Not every stock can be among the highest yielding companies. Sometimes you have to pay up for a company that is simply a juggernaut in its field, and whose financial and operational safety is so strong that a lower current yield is acceptable—especially if you believe you can count on a rising yield during the term of your holding.

This manufacturer of drugs, consumer products, medical devices and instruments, is as wired into every hospital and drugstore in the country as Pitney Bowes is wired into every decent-sized office. As a consequence of their multitude of customer relationships they know what hospitals and doctors need, and they know what the competition is doing in every area of the medical business. Their products are in use every day, and often as not are disposable or consumable. Recessions don't change their business, higher interest rates don't hurt them, storms and earthquakes and pestilence and plagues are only more grist for their mill. Even the emergence of the HMO system hasn't put a dent in the company's profitability.

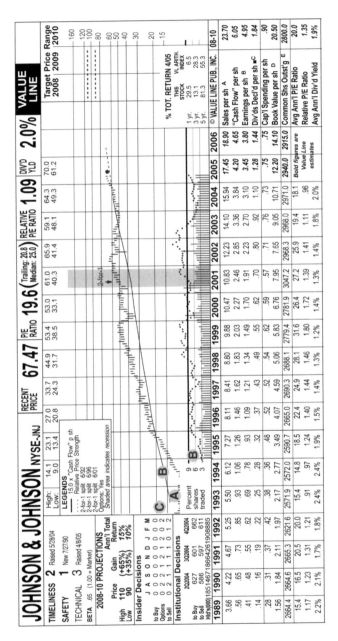

Figure 8-5

Yet even this company can be subject to investor rejection and fear from time to time. In the 1992–93 period, for example, there was nothing wrong with the company's earnings or dividend growth (though it may have missed some analysts' expectations by a penny or two), yet investors managed to sell the stock down to a low that was about 35% from its high. As the current yield approached 3% (which is high for a stock with this kind of growth and reliability combined with A+ financial strength ratings) in 1993 (A) the stock appeared to be a strong long-term buy, priced in the split-adjusted 'teens. As 1994 came into view the stock made a technical "turn," accompanied by rising relative strength (B) after a period of relative weakness (C). The fundamentals clearly remained intact, with rising earnings and dividends all through the stock's two-year price decline. What's not to like? As you'd expect, the dividend nearly doubled and the stock rose a bit more than 100%—in four years.

High quality—a reputable company in its industry with a record of success against formidable competition and diversified against a downturn in any one of its businesses. High financial strength—ratings at the top of the chart, a dividend payout ratio below 40%, profit margins in the mid-teens, retained earnings above 20%. Good current yield—near 3% at its lows, which is not huge but which is good for a stock of such high quality and size. Outstanding growth of yield in excess of 15% per year. What's not to like? Especially during those times when investors' highest hopes are placed elsewhere.

AQUA AMERICA (Figure 8-6). Do you use water every day? Do you pay a water bill every month (if you're a tenant it's built into your rent)? Water is the forgotten utility: ubiquitous, addictive, subject to inelastic demand. And it can provide the foundation for a great reliable growth company when it is a profitable substance marketed and delivered by able management.

After American Water Works (shown in the first edition of this book) was taken over, we sought a similar holding in this field that is uniquely

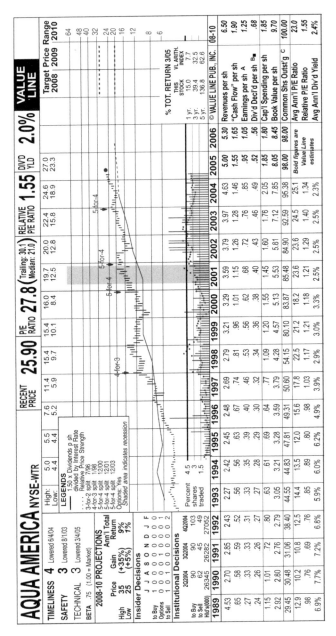

Figure 8-6

monopolistic and which we daresay will never be replaced by a new technology. Aqua America (formerly Philadelphia Suburban) owns and/ or operates under contract water systems around the country. There is no competition, yet the average customer pays them more than $40 per month—more than for basic cable and basic phone service. On average, WTR has been able to earn over 12% annually on equity with clockwork regularity, and, as we know, 12% compounds rather rapidly into very large numbers. It's also spectacular for a company whose customers require its product and which has no competition either for its business or for its product. This is another company with consistent sustainable earnings growth year after year accompanied by commensurate dividend increases.

There's a great "story" for future growth, a kind of "kicker" here as well. The federal Safe Drinking Water Act has mandated a number of expensive changes to water transport and purification systems. While WTR will have to implement these changes on its own systems, it will recover the costs in rates. On the other hand, there are thousands—thousands and thousands—of outdated municipal water systems in this country. The towns and water districts facing upgrades have lots of other needs for funds and for other capital improvements, and many will be inclined to let WTR take over their systems, either as contract operator or as owner. This provides a tremendous field of consolidation opportunity for the company in the years ahead, and management has already shown its ability to wring profits out of the service.

Dividends have doubled and so has the stock since 1999. At a P/E ratio of 28, though, we can hardly say the news is not out. The stock's a bit too high to add here (in 2005), but investors should watch it for any short-term or market-induced dips that would bring it into a better valuation range. One thing is certain: human beings will continue to need clean fresh water.

HEALTHCARE REALTY (Figure 8-7). REITs (Real Estate Investment Trusts) offer investors a high yielding participation in the world of large real estate investors. Bear in mind that REIT dividends are higher than most stocks, but the dividends don't qualify for the 15% tax rate that applies to ordinary dividends of companies that pay normal taxes, since REITs are pass-through entities that don't pay tax at the corporate level.

Because REITs have, like banks, commodity-like characteristics, I prefer REITs at a deep discount or REITs with some kind of specialty niche (these are less likely to be moved by the ebb and flow of sentiment among the various REIT sectors), such as, in this case, the ownership of healthcare properties.

Note that instead of earnings, most REIT analysts focus on Funds From Operations, or FFO (A). In the case of HCR, FFO went flat in 1999 and 2000 (B), despite the company's strong record of prior growth and its consistent and ongoing increases in distributions to investors (C). Clearly, the company didn't feel a need to husband resources and retrench on the distribution front (D), though investors become frightened and drove the stock to a substantial discount to book value. (Actually, in the REIT world asset values are usually measured by Net Asset value, or NAV, though the "book value" numbers that Value Line uses are a reasonable proxy). The ongoing growth of dividends (or distributions) told me that the REITs problems were temporary, and that here was an opportunity to purchase unique assets on sale, at a discount of over 20%. It was merely a matter of sitting after that, while the company recaptured a significant premium and rose by 100% over the next four years (E)—raising distributions all the while. At today's rates, the income yield is about 13% on initial investment, and it continues to rise. The stock is now at a large premium, however, and wouldn't be a buy today (F).

See Appendix B for some of the special considerations regarding analyzing REIT investments.

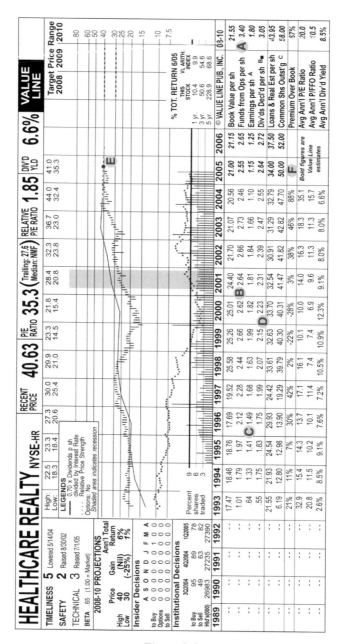

Figure 8-7

KINDER MORGAN ENERGY PARTNERS (FIGURE 8-8). MLPs, or Master Limited Partnerships, are an area that has just come into its own over the past ten years, but they are based on operating assets that are as old as the nation's energy infrastructure, and run by experienced managers. These assets include local and long distance pipelines (for oil, gas, chemicals, and gasoline), processing plants, storage facilities, terminals—all the facilities you need to bring energy from the production fields to the end user. Generally they are mature assets, with relatively slow growth. This maturity, though, is in my mind well offset by the unique character of the assets and by the fact that they are most often quite difficult to replace. In addition, the MLPs themselves are well able to grow as companies through construction of assets and purchases of assets from major oil companies that are refocusing on their core production businesses. In many cases, such as Kinder Morgan Energy Partners, assets are moved from the general partner, which is an operating energy company (like Kinder Morgan, Inc), to a "home" in the MLP.

A major reason for this is the attractive tax picture for MLP investors. Because the companies are able to deduct significant depreciation and depletion tax features, the income investors receive from MLPs is often completely or mostly tax-deferred. You don't pay income tax on this cash flow. Instead your tax cost is reduced by the amount of the distribution, and you pay greater tax—but at the 15% capital gains rate, and only when you sell. If you don't sell, your income is largely tax free for the duration of your holding. The paperwork is a little annoying at tax time, but in my view well worth it.

Indeed, the MLP universe contains a number of stocks with the stellar yield and performance of Kinder Morgan Energy Partners. In my firm we bought the stock as part of a transaction in which we held a company taken over by Kinder Morgan, Inc., at around twelve. At that time the yield on original investment was about 6%. But KMP has been mighty in increasing distributions, which are now up fourfold from the first purchase—in about

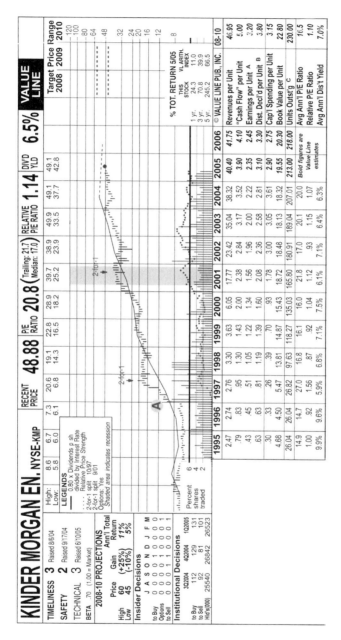

Figure 8-8

seven years! And the stock has kept pace, rising to about fifty as I write. This is pretty much the ultimate yield + yield growth investment: income only return on original investment is nearly 30%! Considering the fact that the stock is also up fourfold, I don't think you can do better, nor should you want to!

Further, the MLPs are ideal for our purposes because they are so transparent. Again, it is a flow-through entity with the focus on cash flow, not earnings, so there are very few ways in which investors can get snookered by management. There have been no scandals in this field—unlike most other industries, and I believe that's a consequence of the basic transparency of the business structure. Don't be put off by the "partnership" aspect of MLPs; they trade mostly on the New York Stock Exchange, with liquidity as high as any other stocks. I like to think of these as utilities with no limit to their upside potential. The key investment statistic is growth in cash flow, and the amount by which the cash flow covers the distribution.

PROCTER AND GAMBLE (FIGURE 8-9). Procter and Gamble is probably the ultimate consumer non-durable stock, making well-known products that we use everyday, from toothpaste to diapers to underarm deodorant, and the company has a substantial division that produces proprietary prescription drugs as well. It is a brand developer almost without peer, and one of the largest advertisers in the mass media. A truly global company, it is almost the definition of a solid moderate earnings and dividend growth stock with proven markets and a reliable future, and an institutional favorite as well due to its enormous size.

But it seems even the Rock of Gibraltar can go on sale from time to time on Wall Street, when suddenly (briefly) investors are apparently able to imagine that the rock may be just ready to crumble into worthless dust. On March 7, 2000 (A), the company announced a 20% decrease to its current quarter earnings guidance because of raw material costs, and the stock, which had been declining for several weeks prior, dropped 31% in price on

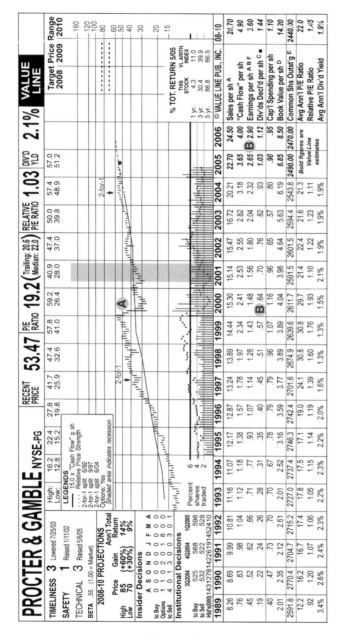

Figure 8-9

a single day, wiping out $35 billion in market cap. This, despite the fact that materials prices clearly go up and down over time, and that the company is well capable of exerting cost control and finding substitutes if materials prices become more permanent. One would imagine that materials costs have gone up and down periodically over the entire life of the company. A true long-term investor can look past these blips and evaluate the company as a total ongoing enterprise, but myopic investors think only: *run!*

And yet, before investors' eyes was a triple-A rated company with thousands of products, a total global distribution system for those products, plants and factories all over the world, 110,000 employees, major brands, and an unblemished record of constantly rising sales, earnings, book value, and dividends. Viewing only the near-term issue of temporary rising costs, investors surely missed the point. This was a tree with the perhaps the longest taproot of any in the forest. Emotionally casting off the shares, sellers created a once-in-a-lifetime bargain sale for buyers whose mentality stretched beyond this quarter's earnings reports and could see the broad outlines of an indefinitely expansive future for this proven enterprise (note the emotionally tell-tale huge increase in volume at the time). Over the next five years earnings and dividend growth retained their historic pattern, the stock price more than doubled off the lows, and dividends rose by more than 60% (B). Today, yield on original investment for a buyer at the lows is about 5% and rising by about 10% per year. Jail is recommended for any investor who desires yet more.

Caveat Emptor

Please bear in mind that, as I noted at the beginning of this chapter, the stocks listed above are not "current recommendations" and you should not purchase them without further investigation of their present circumstances. By the time you read this book it may be a year or more since it was written. "Things change" is a truth of the marketplace, though we've done our best in this book to focus on what are certain eternal verities—as far as we know. The examples above are just that: *examples*, to help you learn how to look for and think about Single Best Investment stocks. I think the text makes clear that these are certainly good stocks to review but, again, the current circumstances need to be right. For example, as I write the market is rather richly valued. I'd pay more heed now to *high current yield* with a bit of modest growth—since a high yield can provide a cushion against downside volatility—than to any promises of great future growth. At a time when the market has been in a tailspin, however, one might want to pay more attention to stocks that have continued to grow well as companies, despite a falling stock price.

chapter 9

HOW TO HOLD AND WHEN TO SELL: ATTITUDE IS EVERYTHING

People have a way of looking at me strangely when I tell them that long-term investing isn't about having a great system, or a superior analytic intellect, or better access to information, or even the best advice money can buy. Long-term investing is about character, about depth of vision and the cultivation of patience, about who you are and who you've made yourself to be.

For all good things come from having the vision to see how a company's story will unfold in the future, having the patience to let it unfold, having the generosity of spirit to have faith in management to do the job for you, the passive investor. Having the good sense to understand that you *are* a passive investor, an investor in a company with factories or facilities, workers, decision makers, financiers, other shareholders—an investor in all this, not an investor in a name with a number that bounces up and down in the newspaper each day.

In some ways, the Single Best Investment strategy is an antidote. For what ails investors is not so much a lack of the necessary intelligence to identify a company that might do well in the future (although I must confess that the majority of stocks often make me wonder, *who owns this junk?*), but an inability to see the far horizon of compounded growth, and a consequent inability to have a really comfortable and satisfying relationship with a particular investment.

Too Many Stimuli

The emotional odds are stacked against the shareholder. There are constant voices attempting to seduce you from your path and take you onto another. There is the voice of insecurity about your view of the long-term strategy of a company. Do you really know enough to know that the company has a good plan? If you're wrong will your money just drizzle away year after year, or go up in a poof of smoke? Similarly, paranoia often enters. Did your broker get an extra commission for putting you in this thing? Is management just pumping the stock up so they can sell out themselves at a nice price? Is this another BRE-X Minerals, with frauds and suicide and who knows what else all dedicated to kiting the stock price? What about that rumor reported in *Investor's Daily?* Is that for real, or just generated by short sellers?

And then, as Mick Jagger once said so eloquently, a "man comes on the radio, and he's telling me more and more, about some useless information, supposed to fire my imagination, I can't get no, oh no no no!" In Jagger's case he couldn't get no satisfaction. In the investor's case, he can't get no peace and quiet, nor peace of mind, tranquility, nor a sense that the decision made was the right one and one worth sticking by through thick and thin until the final tale is told. It's hard. Here you are sitting on a nice income-producing solid company with a fifty-year history of modest success, and out pops this IPO stacked like a Playboy bunny which promptly doubles in a week. Your old field hand is still just wheezing higher in dimes and quarters. Gee, shouldn't you be thinking about planting some of that greener grass?

The emotions of a holder can be your undoing. The rules for picking a Single Best Investment stock aren't that hard. What's hard is keeping your mind on your wife when you're a judge at the Miss Universe pageant. Here come all the beautiful alternatives, each with their corps of press agents and managers and media patsies ready to tell you why this one, of all the possibles, is the one that's really better than sliced bread. You can't pick up a newspaper or magazine or watch TV without some highly credible sales type telling you in the most confidential tones why you should like this one and not that one, why that one and not this one. It is a steady stream of noise, and just when that noise has died down you bump into a friend who can't wait to regale you with stories of all the wonderful stocks he bought just three months ago. How is it, I often wonder, that none of my friends has ever bought a loser? It's amazing. Why don't they tell me about all these winners right when they're buying them? I sure would like to "get in on" the ones they tell me they "got in on." And how come they're still commuting to work, anyway, with all these big hits bulging up their trading accounts?

Easy In, Easy Out

But the worst thing isn't just the ecosystem of information, opinion, and the Three Sirens (greed, fear, conformity) that constitute our environment. The worst thing is that very feature which is supposed to be best, which is supposed to distinguish our domestic market as the best in the world, the best in the history of man. The worst thing is the almost infinite liquidity of the market, and constant transparency of prices. These two features, which every Nobel prizewinning economist will agree are the key features underpinning a modern, democratic, rational, and enlightened marketplace, are the undoing of most investors.

The fabulous liquidity of our markets means you can get in or out of a stock in literally thirty seconds. It becomes terribly easy to act on a passing emotion or an incorrect and hasty reaction to a piece of corporate news.

Although you may have started your investment with a long-term idea, with an idea of commitment and perseverance as a way, if nothing else, to avoid the mistakes that come from precipitous judgment, you're in a situation where the mechanism for entry and exit encourages quick, not circumspect, action. In fact, that's how brokers often make their money, by encouraging action in a context that makes action easy—adding yet another impetus to what one might call the "exercise of liquidity." Something akin to an inalienable right. It's just too darn easy to pick up the phone and change your position.

Imagine if divorce just required filling out a two-line form and dropping it off at Town Hall. How many intact marriages do you think we'd have? Imagine if selling a house was as easy as selling a thousand shares of Microsoft. Wouldn't houses turn over much faster? Imagine any relationship, marriage or any other, that you can just terminate with a phone call and have no further apparent present-time consequences. Or, for that matter, imagine being able to start a relationship with just a phone call. We know instinctively there should be more, there should be depth, there should be familiarity.

Liquidity permits you to float, unfocused, like a cork among the lily pads, tossing this way and that with every passing breeze. It focuses your mind on the *possible*—since, after all, with total liquidity any move is possible to make—and **distracts you from the disciplined commitment you've made to the principal of compounding,** an abstraction which you don't always feel as it's happening. You more likely feel the pressures of conflicting information and opinion each day. These are easier to feel, and often wind up seeming more real, than the slow and inexorable underground process of compounding.

The "system" makes it easy for you to generate a commission. It makes it easy for you to make a decision, or relieve yourself of anxiety. The system brings you into the churn, like a bit of flotsam swirling down into a whirlpool. Only in this case it doesn't feel like a whirlpool, because you feel, and you're made to feel, like a responsible grown-up doing adult things with your money which is yours and you own it and nobody can do anything with it except for you and you can make any decision you want. You feel *important,* making financial decisions, and you feel it **is** important to make financial decisions. Like a high roller who's given free things in Vegas, the house will do everything it can to accommodate you—and keep you at the tables...

To Have and to Hold

The hard part in investing is holding, and learning to tolerate the myriad and relentless swings of greed and fear to which an investment holder is inevitably subject. But unless you control these impulses—and we all feel them, all who "hold" must feel them—you won't reach your ultimate goals. And your ultimate goals are simple, as we've defined them many times in this book: *to get an excellent return on your invested capital with as little anxiety as possible by making maximum use of the principal of compounding, and by investing in stocks whose chief appeal is as vehicles in a compounding process, or "parts" of a compounding machine.*

Holding successfully requires a kind of spartan attitude, a kind of warrior attitude, in which you hold your ground, never tromping away, through thick and thin, through storms and sun, never becoming excessively excited or happy by profitable rallies, never sinking into gloom or depression or second thoughts when prices are on the wane. A warrior attitude in which feelings may be felt, even deeply felt, but not necessarily acted out. As William Blake put it in rather a different context, in *The Marriage of Heaven and Hell,* "Joy laughs not! Sorrows weep not!"

As a warrior you understand that there are many ways to win the battle of investing, there are many ways to come out on top in the end. But some ways are wiser than others, designed to maintain sanity in a chaotic world. The warrior attitude says: this is my strategy. It is a good one. It will work. I will not deviate from it no matter what the seeming success in the moment of some other strategy or approach. I will see to the other side; I will recognize that the candle which burns the brightest also burns away the quickest.

A warrior will continually remind himself through examination of historical results that the path of quality and yield is unassailable, and shines with increasing superiority the longer the period of comparison becomes. Arms folded, feet squarely on the ground, the winds may blow around the warrior's head, but they serve only to cool his blood. He casts a cold objective eye on his companies, their long-term promise and their short-term progress, and a still and silent eye on the machinations of others in the market. The sun sets and the warrior-investor's silhouette is traced in the colored and darkening sky. In the morning he stands where he stood the evening before, unchanging, glittering in the morning sunlight.

All night long he has been focused on compounding and logic, and the logic of compounding. It is the logic of compounding that is his mantra, his mantra to enlightenment. Over and over he remembers: *"rising income will ultimately produce rising prices commensurate with the rising income. If the income doubles, the stock will double. Often it will more than double, as the stock comes back into investors' favor. But logic says it will double at least.. Even if a stock's price were to remain unchanged for decades, the rising income would ultimately give me annual returns from income alone that are higher than the historic average returns expectable from the stock indices."*

It's the logic of compounding and the unfolding of history that's your "bet" when you invest in high-quality high-yield high-growth-of-yield stocks. It's *time* that you're investing in, really, time and the notion that over time the economy and the companies that serve the economy will grow at least modestly. Rather than being "in the market" you're taking advantage of an unheralded opportunity that the market offers: ironically, it's an opportunity to pursue an investment strategy that really has very little to do with the market. It has everything to do with simple arithmetic, and the simple principle of moderate growth derived from doing basic business. The warrior mentality will continually remember these principles of investment, and use them to ward off the slings and arrows of uncertainty and influence that are a constant nemesis. They will be the investor's garlic against the Dracula of the market environment and the market circumstances. When driving at 6 p.m. and the nightly news comes on the radio ("telling me more and more, about some useless information"), a warrior investor will simply look out at the landscape, unmoved, when the daily change in the Dow Jones Industrials is announced. The most active list? It's sort of dull and boring. It's got new names every day.

So stop looking at the market! Stop paying close attention to the price changes, the opinions, the mavens, the gurus, the new highs, the IPOs, the mergers, the takeovers, the LBOs , the CMOs, The Ginnie Maes, the Freddie Macs, the Federal Reserve, the program trades. Forget it, forget the whole throbbing beehive. Take a long trip to an undeveloped third world country, and don't come back for months! Let the compounding do its work. Let management be your employees!

That's how to hold!

The Real Estate Paradigm—A Landlord's Attitude

Now that you've got the right "holding head," let's come back down to earth, because not all problems are solved by affirmations or visions of inner strength. What you need to do, to be successful as a holder, is to envision your stock holdings as similar—very, very, similar—to another investment that you probably know something about and have probably experienced as a holder: *real estate.*

What do you look for when buying a piece of real estate? You want a good location, of course, but first and foremost when buying a piece of income property, you want it to pay the bills and leave you some cash return on your investment. If it looks as though it needs too much repair, you won't buy it (unless the price is really cheap). If it's in a really risky neighborhood, you probably won't buy it (unless it's really *really* cheap!).

You want to own something that's going to pay its own bills and give you a cash return on your investment right away. You know that over the years you'll be able to raise the rents—maybe more than normal if you do some refurbishing—and over the years the cash return you earn will go higher and higher.

And you know that income real estate is valued on a multiple of its rents (ten times rent in a great neighborhood, five times rent if a large community fire is possible during the summer). As the rents go up, so does the value of the property. And, if you get lucky, maybe the neighborhood suddenly becomes very popular, or IBM builds a new plant nearby, and your property rises even more than the rents rise.

How do you hold an income property, property that is not traded round the clock like stocks, whose prices are not always known and available, like stocks, and where you can't just pick up the phone and transact with a buyer, as you can with stocks? How do you hold this other vehicle that embodies the principal of financial compounding?

First of all, you *don't* check the prices every day, or even every week, or even every month. You might note with interest from time to time how properties are trading in your market, but that's about it. You don't rush to sell when prices change. You don't listen to the evening news and figure the worth of your property on a running basis. You sit with your property. You know that rents will rise as leases come due, and that if you hold on your property will slowly appreciate in value over time. If you're managing your property you look for ways to enhance its value, and if you've got a manager working for you to manage the property you evaluate regular reports to ensure that steady progress is being made.

You take a long view, knowing that you've made an investment, not a trade, and that your investment was made with a fully realized vision of how the future will unfold. There are, of course, no guarantees that the future will unfold as you've planned it, but you also know that the investment will ripen, assuming it does ripen, in its time, over time. You don't expect to turn around and sell your property tomorrow, or next week, or next month, or next year. In fact, if the building continues to make money and the rents continue to rise, you might well want to own it for your entire life.

Why should a stock investment be any different? It isn't, really. The fact that you have access to so much information, and that everyone in the world including your Uncle Louie has an opinion on what you've invested in and what you should invest in, is what makes it seem different. The ecosystem of stocks includes tremendous and subtle pressures to transact, when in fact the big rewards all come from holding. Even the famous speculator Jesse Livermore said, "I made all my money from sitting." How does Warren Buffett make his money? "While I'm snoring," he says.

The Right Way to Monitor Your Stocks

Focus on your compounding machine, not the constantly fluctuating prices of things (what's that old saying about the person who knows the price of everything and the value of nothing?). Not the machine-gun firing of information, incessant information, about companies. And, above all, steer your gaze clear of the hot items of the moment, of all stocks, really, that are not the ones you hold. To be sure, you will always want to be on the lookout for candidates, and some candidates may even prove to be better ideas than your holdings, but always, always, look only at the stocks that fit within your discipline, your discipline of 1) high quality, 2) high current yield, and 3) rising income.

Your job as a holder is to monitor your positions quarterly to determine whether each stock is performing its function as a part in a compounding machine. You'll want to look at the company's quarterly reports for this. You'll want to see that earnings are roughly what's necessary for the company to both pay the current dividend and to increase it when appropriate.

You'll want to see that revenues are rising (unless a division has been sold off or spun off), for revenues are the raw material from which companies can make profits, and profits cannot be spun up from thin air without revenues—cost cutting can often help the bottom line, but the benefits of cost cutting only last so long in the absence of increased revenues. You'll want to see that the company's business plan is consistent with the plan that was in effect when you purchased, and that company developments are consistent with the "story" that convinced you to choose this one from among the field of Single Best Investment candidates.

If the "story" was steady growth based on good demographic trends, be sure you see that growth is present, and not a perpetual promise for the future. If the story involved an exciting diversification built on top of good cash flow, make sure that both elements are showing progress.

Did the company miss analysts' earnings targets by a penny or two? Forget about it. The analysts' projections are notoriously unstable and inaccurate. (David Dreman once did a statistical study which showed that the odds of an analyst correctly predicting company earnings each quarter for five years were worse than ten million to one!) Earnings should not be on a consistent downtrend, but companies often have a quarter or several quarters of stagnant or soft earnings—especially when building up a new line or expanding the business to bring in future profits—and it's no cause for alarm. In general, you need to become passive: let management do its job. Once you've become involved in a stock, consider management your employees. If they've done well in the past, they're likely to do well again in the future, even if for a quarter to two they don't seem to have that old pizzazz. Remember, these are not stocks where the world is waiting with bated breath for the next earnings announcement. These are stocks that are priced on intrinsic value, on long-term earning power, not the details of moment-to-moment growth. The market won't be spooked by minor disappointments, and you shouldn't be either.

Dividends: Always the Key

However, as a holder you do need to be especially alert to the state of the dividend. As you surely know by now, we consider the dividend to be the litmus test for a dividend-paying company. It is like a cardiogram image of the heartbeat, or breath on the mirror. No matter what the earnings picture may look like, no matter what Wall Street analysts or talking heads on TV may say, the dividend is the tell-tale. If the company has a history of raising dividends and the dividend doesn't rise within about a year when it should (and there's no excuse such as a big capital expenditure), something's wrong.

Any company is complex, and there are, therefore, many issues surrounding each company, issues that can provide fodder for sports fans to debate the merits until the wee hours of the morning. But our strategy is based on a simple principle—that each stock can provide an instance of the compounding principle. And that's all we want from a stock. We don't care if its chairman makes the cover of *Time,* or if management gets the national Award of Excellence, or if company headquarters are designed by the world's greatest architect or a local building contractor (actually, the latter is to be favored in most cases). What we care about is that the company can participate as a "part" in a portfolio that is a long-term compounding machine. We never want to take our eyes off that one-and-only concept.

This means that <u>what you really must know</u>—and *all* you really must know—is what's happening with the dividend. There are four questions regarding the dividend:

1. *Is the dividend in jeopardy?* This is basically the payout ratio question. As we discussed when looking at the payout ratio (the ratio of dividend to total earnings), for ordinary industrial companies it should be no higher than 50%. It can be higher for utilities and REITs. If the payout ratio is more than 50%, look to the past history of the company; for some companies it's normal to have a higher payout ratio, and if that's true, then there's no problem. In some cases the payout ratio suddenly rises because reported earnings are low due to write-offs or some other kind of one-time event. If a high ratio can be explained as due to one-time occurrences or expenses, you're still okay. Cash flow and revenues should still be level or higher if this is the case, however. Look as well at the trend of the payout ratio. If it's been declining there should be no cause for worry, since increasing earnings in future years will cause the ratio to decline yet further. The problem area is when a payout ratio rises without explanation and without the security of an accompanying increase in revenues and/or cash flow. At some point the company will be unable to increase the dividend, and the company will no longer be playing its appointed role in our compounding game.

2. *Has the company changed its dividend policy?* Most companies maintain a policy of paying out, say, 30% or 40% of earnings in dividends. If the company announces that the policy has been revised so that a lesser percentage of earnings will be paid out, the chances of a dividend increase diminish. The company becomes a problematic holding.

3. *Has the company failed to raise its dividend for one year?* Sometimes, as noted above, there's an excuse. It might be a capital construction

program or, in the case of a utility, it might even be unusual weather. But whatever the reason, failure to raise the dividend is a red flag for any of our holdings. You need to evaluate the overall circumstances further. If the reason for a failure to raise relates to spending in order to have greater revenues in the future, or there's a clear excuse, you need not worry. But if there's been a history of increases, and now there's no increase, and there is only silence regarding the reasons behind the change, it may be time to look for a new "part" for your compounding machine. Generally, we will not hold a stock more than two years without a dividend increase, unless there are clear and articulated mitigating circumstances.

4. *Has the company cut its dividend?* Dividend cuts are the kiss of death for stock pricing generally, and are a direct contradiction of the principles that guide a Single Best Investment portfolio generally. You should really never get to the point where your stock cuts the dividend by surprise (rising payout ratios, falling earnings accompanied by falling revenues, company statements, all should key you in to the possibility of a cut long before it happens), but if it happens you need to just take your lumps and move on. If the dividend is a flag signaling company health, a cut is a flag at half-mast.

So, unlike many other strategies, we are guided in our holding periods and holding attitudes by *corporate dividend behavior and the corporate dividend situation*. We bought our stocks for current income and growth of income, the growth of income being the underlying force responsible for future appreciation of the stock. If the company fails to raise its dividend on a regular and predictable basis, it's no longer useful in our particular portfolio. There may be many other investors who will want a given stock for any of a myriad of different reasons. And that's good. Because you will have buyers to whom you can sell the misbehaving "part" of your compounding machine.

As a corollary, as long as the stock is providing the features for which you bought it, you will want to hold it. Don't be led astray by the noise of the investment world, or the need for novelty, or the feeling that the grass might be greener someplace else. Every decision provides an opportunity to be wrong, so the fewer decisions you make, the better off you are. If you're uncertain about a stock even though it has been regularly increasing its dividends at an above-average rate, think about taking a Caribbean cruise for ten or twenty weeks. By the time you return, the stock will likely be higher. Seriously, try to forget about your holdings as long as they are doing their job. The more you think about them, the more you ruminate, the more you're likely to seek relief from anxiety in a decision to act. But don't! Remember your place. You're a passive investor. When all is going as you planned it, above all, stay passive!

If the dividend is at risk, or it doesn't grow and there's no excuse, then you may make use of that infinite liquidity in our markets, pick up the phone, and **sell.**

Other Reasons to Sell, All or Part

The only other time to sell would be when a stock spikes upward in price—perhaps on takeover rumors—to the point where its current yield is small in relation to other available stocks. Sophisticated investors may want to consider selling when a stock gets "ahead of itself," but this is a tricky area indeed. How high is too high for a great company over the long term? I don't think anyone can really say, and certainly not an amateur or part-time investor. When a stock spikes it will probably come back down, since stocks tend to regress to the mean of the average annual returns, but, on the other hand, when a stock spikes it's normally because there's something appealing that's newly recognized about it, or something new about the company that investors perceive as adding future value to the stock.

There's a useful old expression which helps resolve this: "you'll never go broke taking a little profit." Consider a partial sale if your stock gets out of hand, bringing it back down to an equal dollar weight with your other stocks.

What if you find an overwhelmingly fine qualifying candidate that you don't own. That might be a reason sell all or part of a holding, to raise cash for the purchase. But, basically, the goal of this program is to try to hold your stocks indefinitely. These are not stocks that are bought to be sold. They're bought because you want to own a slice of this business that grows moderately over the years and shares some if its wealth annually with its owners, the shareholders. When there's a serious question about whether it can continue to do so, as measured by the dividend and the dividend's overall situation, then you may contemplate terminating your status as a holder.

In the meantime, attitude is everything. And the right attitude is unwavering commitment, confident vision in the rising-income future, and a passive embrace of the management that's working for you, a kind of dumb acceptance of the truism that the future will be something like the past, until proven otherwise.

Summing Up:

1. The strategy provides a framework, but true success depends upon maintaining a calm and passive attitude.
2. Emotions and unnecessary decisions are the undoing of most investors.
3. Liquidity, which enables you to make instant decisions, can be a threat to your circumspection.
4. Hold your stocks with a cold, objective eye, an eye fixed on the far horizon.

5. Hold as you would hold real estate.
6. Sell if it appears the dividend may not be increased, or if too much time passes without an increase and there's no legitimate excuse for a failure to increase.

chapter 10

BUILDING YOUR PORTFOLIO

In a way, knowing which SBI stocks we want to buy and hold is just an intermediate step. The next step, and one that's as important as knowing what stocks to buy, is understanding how to put them together.

Asset Allocation

In the investment world today there is one buzzword (and by buzzword I mean "substitute for thought or analysis") that is, to paraphrase Saddam Hussein, the mother of all buzzwords. It's two words, actually, but two words typically spoken as one and with a reverence seen otherwise only in discussions of utmost theological urgency: "asset allocation."

The purveyors of this term will tell you that there are a broad number of different so-called asset classes, that these asset classes behave in different ways at different times, that we can never know ahead of time which of these asset classes will be "the best" in the future—and that the proper way to construct a portfolio is to acquire assets in all the classes in varying proportions. In this way, the theory goes, "risk" is diminished (risk here means both volatility and the "risk" of not being invested in a top-performing asset class), and returns will be good in an average sort of way.

It is very similar to saying you can never really know who's going to win a horse race, so you should buy a ticket on all the horses. You'll always have a winner—though your winners will be mostly offset by your losers. Of course my analogy is extreme. The great thing about investing as a speculative enterprise is that you never lose all your money in an investment as you might in a horse race (certainly not if you adhere to the precepts in this book). Nevertheless, the asset-allocation mentality is rather aligned, in my mind, with the gambler who bets every number.

And that's sad, because it's clearly possible to apply intelligence and eliminate certain asset classes from consideration either permanently or at particular times. Blind adherence to asset allocation normally takes little account of relative valuations, either. Asset allocators will assert that you should have, for example, 50% growth stocks and 50% value stocks in the stock section of your allocation—without ever bothering to attempt to discern whether those two categories are especially cheap or dear at the moment.

One of the things that really undermines the concept here is that most asset allocators include fixed income as an asset class—presumably, the fact that it exists means it should be included. Worse, nearly all practitioners are familiar with the Ibbotson chart of long-term returns from a number of key asset classes that was displayed in Chapter 1. No need to flip back there. I'll refresh your memory. You don't make any money in bonds, and in many if not most periods your returns are actually negative after adjusting for inflation. Unless the world turns upside down in the next fifty years and all becomes its opposite, you should not have any bonds in your portfolio.

The SBI portfolio can do everything that a full-blown asset allocation portfolio can do, and it can do it all in one portfolio—not some far-flung collection of rogue mutual funds or private managers together with the enterprise necessary to find and manage them. This is, after all, the whole point. The menu of investment options and even the array of *de riguer* inclusions has become dizzying, maddening, chaotic, and, worst of all, disturbing. It turns an investor into a frightened bureaucrat. My sandwich board says this: you only need one account with one type of stock—the SBI stock—to accomplish all the goals of a multivariate asset allocation.

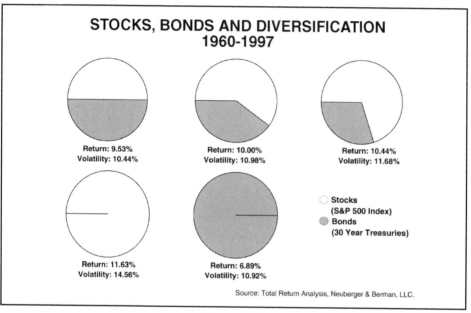

Figure 10-1

Here's what a typical asset allocator might like to see for a fairly high net worth individual of average age and average financial needs and average volatility tolerance. Indeed, there are even some "classic" asset allocations in the investment world. We'll call the client "age fifty executive, conservative but likes to speculate 'just a little,' saving for retirement, would like some current income to pay for ski vacations to Colorado for his family and to help cover his mortgage, which is just a little too big for his budget."

The normal allocation would look like this:

1. Fixed Income: 40%
2. Stocks: 60%
   Large and Medium Stocks.......60%
   Small Stocks.........................20%
   International.........................20%

In other words, 36% of the total portfolio (60% of a 60% equity allocation) would be domestic large and medium capitalization stocks, 12% would be small-cap stocks (20% of 60%), and 12% would be international stocks. Obviously, these percentages would change if the balance between equity and fixed income were changed.

Here's what an overall portfolio would look like in terms of its portfolio characteristics, given the above asset allocation, where "market" equals the S&P 500:

Yield	> market
Price/Book	< market
Expected Return	< market
Expected Volatility	< market
Capitalization Size	< market
Industry Diversity	> or = market ?

The last item includes a question mark because everything depends upon which stocks you would use to fulfill the stock mandate. Presumably, the large and midcaps would reflect the various industries in the index, and the inclusion of small-caps and international would add a level of diversity beyond the index. Likewise, the inclusion of small-caps would almost inevitably mean that the average cap size will be less than the index.

To create this portfolio would require _at least five_ sub-portfolios (funds, private managers, groups of stock selections, or a combination), and in practice would probably involve more than five, since most fixed-income allocations are also broken down into shorter and longer term income instruments. The costs and complications of this set-up are substantial.

But look at how you might accomplish the same thing in a single SBI account, that is, your portfolio of SBI stocks:

Yield	> market
Price/Book	< market
Expected Return	= market
Expected Volatility	< market
Capitalization Size	< market
Industry Diversity	= market ?

The primary difference, on these general categories of portfolio characteristic, is that the SBI portfolio is expected to generate long-term returns about equal to the market, where the asset-allocation portfolio is not, because it includes fixed income.

This is important. To the extent that you include fixed income, you are almost guaranteeing that the portfolio will underperform the market over the long term, because the long-term returns from fixed income are so far below those of equities.

But fixed income dampens volatility and adds cash flow, right? The counter-answer, the SBI answer, and I believe the correct answer, is that you can achieve both without resorting to fixed income and without diminishing returns.

Let's look at a "balanced" asset allocation of stocks and bonds as of 12/31/97 versus an actual Single Best Investment portfolio:

Table 10-1

FACTOR	ASSET ALLOCATION	SBI
Sub-Accounts	5 or more	1
% Yield (60% S&P and 40% Int. Bond)	3.25	5.50
Portfolio Beta	.8	.7
% Expected Return	7.8	11
% Expected Volatility	13	12
% Small Caps	12	12
% International	12	12
% Large & Mid	36	76

As you can see, the net result of a full-blown asset allocation scheme does not bring you any more from a final portfolio than can be accomplished from a single SBI account. In both cases, of course, you can tweak the percentages to suit your taste, your risk tolerances, or your investment outlook. You could easily have 20% international in your SBI portfolio, for example, as well as in your asset allocation portfolio.

But despite the fact that the two portfolios can display almost identical risk characteristics in terms of how much they are likely to fluctuate, the SBI portfolio will inevitably return more over time because it does not contain the "dead" money of fixed income, which can never appreciate.

To some extent, this idea that portfolios can be "balanced" with fixed income comes from lessons learned in ancient history. Once upon a time, bonds did indeed fluctuate very little, because interest rates fluctuated very little. Back then, you were at least fairly certain to dampen the volatility of a portfolio with bonds, if you were willing to give up some return in exchange. In the late 1970s however, the Federal Reserve Board decided to let interest rates "float," and you can see from the chart on page 8 what that has done to bond volatility. Bonds are still a bit less volatile than stocks, but not by much. And their returns are impoverished relative to stocks. Too, most people ignore the fact that the most normal state of affairs in the markets is for bonds and stocks to be moving higher or lower *in tandem*. If that's the case, and if bonds are now much closer to stock volatility, we have to ask if the ancient ideas of the role of bonds still hold any water.

Review the chart on page 8—bond and stock volatility has been similar since the late 1970s. There is nothing to gain from bonds in terms of safety or reduction of fluctuations, and everything to lose in terms of returns.

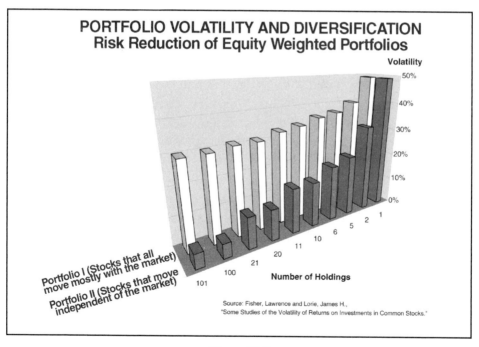

Figure 10-2

Many investors would also be surprised to learn that the *yields* on T-bills have, over the last twenty years, showed more volatility than the stock market. I don't mean to imply that T-bill principal values have fluctuated more than stocks or at all, but the percentage change in *yields* has been radical, to say the least. Less than twenty years ago T-bills might yield 15% or more, while today they yield 5%. For the bill to rise from 5% to 7%, an easily imagined movement, will involve a yield change of no less than 40%!

How Many Stocks?

In our portfolios for individuals and institutions we tend to carry thirty to forty stocks (except for one high-income strategy). That may be a large number for an individual investor to both identify and track, though it's about the smallest number of stocks that I'm personally comfortable with in terms of a portfolio that's not going to fluctuate as much as the overall market. And it's a small number for most institutional clients.

The rule on this is simple, and it's the rule that underlies Modern Portfolio Theory: the fewer stocks you have the more likely you are to experience greater volatility than the market, and the more stocks you have the less likely you are to experience greater volatility. The more stocks you have, the more your group will behave like the index. However, there is a threshold above which the reduction in volatility isn't significant—historic performance of the Dow Jones Industrials has shown that level to be around thirty issues of good quality and large size. Since smaller stocks tend to be more volatile, you'll need more than thirty stocks in a portfolio to approximate market volatility, unless the stocks you choose tend to be individually less volatile, which is the case with SBI stocks.

This is a pretty simple concept when viewed at the logical extreme. Let's say you owned all five hundred stocks in the S&P 500, at the same weights as their representation in the S&P 500. Obviously, your portfolio would move in lockstep with the index, because it would, in fact, be the index. As you move away from the structure of the index, with fewer stocks, you run an increasing "risk" of increasing what students in the field call your "risk"— your volatility. You could, of course, hold only the least volatile stocks in the index, letting go of the jumpiest items. In that case your volatility would be different from the index and probably lower than the average.

The volatility-reduction effect of diversifying a portfolio has been studied by academics. Evans and Archer found that about 90% of the maximum benefit was achieved using a portfolio of twelve to eighteen stocks. That study was undertaken in 1968, when there were far fewer issues. In 1987 Meir Statman published work that indicated that a well-diversified portfolio must contain at least thirty stocks. To some extent the number of stocks you hold will depend on your comfort level and your ability to both find and follow suitable holdings. But remember, if you hold five good-quality utility stocks, all five are likely to move in the same direction at the same time. In terms of the benefits of diversification, your goal should be to include different kinds of companies in different industries.

If you want to hold a smaller portfolio but you still want to have volatility that's less than the market, the stocks you hold in a smaller portfolio need to be *less volatile and more conservative* than the average of all the stocks in the index. The smaller your portfolio, the more conservative should your stocks be, if you want to maintain low volatility. Of course SBI stocks satisfy this requirement on all fours, which is why I don't really feel the need for a portfolio of one hundred or two hundred stocks or more, as you might see in some mutual funds.

If you don't want to hold the thirty to forty stocks that satisfy my personal comfort level, you can reduce the number—bearing in mind that each reduction increases the risk that a single bad apple in your bushel will have an excessive impact on results. I think ten stocks are too few, if you want to have adequate diversification among industries, cap size, and nationality.

Fifteen to twenty carefully chosen stocks will probably provide enough diversification to achieve the goals of an SBI strategy—the Evan and Archer study supports this view (more importantly, my own real world experience supports it as well). That's fewer than are in the Dow Jones Industrial Average (thirty), but when you consider that the DJI is no more volatile than the S&P 500 the smaller number shouldn't be too frightening.

There are certain categories that lend stability to a portfolio without compromising return, and I recommend that you include as much of these as you would include of fixed income in a "balanced" portfolio. In other words, about half your portfolio should be composed of real estate, utilities, MLPs, and the highest yielding industrial stocks that are also high quality dividend-growth items. Some of these higher-yielding items might be foreign utilities. In any event, experience has taught me that positions should always be equal-weighted, since you never know in advance which will be the best and worst stocks. A sixteen-stock portfolio as of 2005 might look like this:

6% Telfonica de Mexico	Utility, foreign
6% Energy East	Utility
6% Boston Properties	Real Estate
6% Campbell Soup	Consumer, Food&Bev
6% MDU Resources	Utility
6% Pitney Bowes	Office Products
6% U.S. Bancorp	Finance
6% Enterprise Products	Energy (MLP)
6% Bank of America	Finance
6% Fidelity National	Finance
6% ING	Finance, foreign
6% BP	Energy, foreign
6% Procter and Gamble	Consumer
6% Landaur	Ind. Service, small
6% Emerson Electric	Cap Goods

| 6% Johnson and Johnson | Health |
| 4% Cash | *awaiting investment* |

If you want technology exposure, add a tech mutual fund—you'll not find many SBI candidates in the Technology sector. This portfolio carries a current yield of about 4%—about the same right now, as the 10-year bonds (future readers may be surprised to read that!), and it is fully capable of returning more than 20% in any given year, with the absolute minimum of downside risk should things turn melancholy in the overall market. Note that at 4% the portfolio yield is 2.4 times as much as the S&P 500 and should be much less risky than the index even though it contains such a small number of stocks.

You can have even fewer stocks, but if you do you should apply the same logic: *the fewer stocks you hold, the more conservative each issue should be*.

Weighting

Observe that the stocks in the above portfolio are held at equal dollar weighting. That's the rule. Why? Sad to say, you never really know in advance which will be the best and which will be the worst (if you did, you'd only buy the best!). We've found that equal dollar weighting is the appropriate way to run a portfolio, no matter how many stocks are held. If you want to hold fifty stocks, each will be weighted at 2% of the total dollars. As noted above, the fewer stocks you hold, the more conservative each individual issue should be (i.e., it should have high yield, low beta, stable business, low debt or debt appropriate for its industry).

One last note: the portfolio above is just a sample, just an example. Much may have changed for any one of the stocks mentioned by the time you read this book, so even if this "menu" whets your appetite you'd better check to see that all the ingredients are fresh.

What About Cash?

In general, most studies have shown that remaining fully invested at all times is the most likely way to generate gains that are closest to the index (since the index is always fully invested), but this old saw could use some oiling and sharpening. The problem with "stay fully invested" as an investment conclusion is the same as with many investment conclusions: we simply don't have enough data to know if that's a valid statement.

Virtually every study you will see in support of the "stay invested" school of thought relies on twenty years or less of data. It is generally accepted among statisticians that we need at least one hundred observations to draw a statistically valid conclusion, so this and most other investment shibboleths you will hear are worthy of some measure of skepticism or suspicion up front. But worse, most who advise full investment are basing their conclusion on the past twenty years or so, when we have been experiencing the greatest bull market of all time! Even if you look further back, all you see is bull market bull market bull market, with brief and well-known exceptions, for the bulk of the twentieth century (and there is little good data earlier than 1900).

Nevertheless, I agree that "full investment" (more than 90% of the portfolio) should be the policy of your portfolio, though for somewhat different reasons. Rather than a policy which attempts to be clever vis a vis the stock market, a notion of full investment has much more to do with being a real investor, a real partner in a business that is going to bring your real long-term returns from its real long-term steady and sustainable growth. This growth—and growth of the dividends you're paid—comes in small increments. You can't just dip in one day for some growth and then go away until the next time you need a dose. Partners are partners, like mates in a marriage. To get the full benefit of the intimacy, wisdom, and depth that the years bring, the partners have to stay together. Obviously, in the investment world polygamy is both acceptable and beneficial, but to each mate you must make a real commitment if you want to see the good things that time, and only time, can bring.

What About Higher Income?

There's a saying in the investment world that may likely be as old as civilization itself: "there's room in business for bulls and bears, but hogs eventually get slaughtered." The investor commonly known as a "yield hog" typically comes to a bad end. For the simple fact is that the old expression "if it looks too good to be true, it probably is," has a great deal of currency. But it is still possible to invest "for yield" using Single Best Investment stocks and maintain a portfolio that offers income as high as bonds *without giving up* the growth of yield we consider so important, or the chance for capital appreciation.

The construction of a portfolio involves a constant interplay between the need for yield (or the security that yield provides) and the need for inflation-beating appreciation. In most cases there's a "trade-off" between yield and growth, but that's not the same as saying there's a "trade away." I write these words fresh from gains at our firm of 26% in 2003 and 15% in 2004 from our highest-yielding portfolio. Extremely conservative stocks can do extremely well, surprisingly well: one shouldn't be shy about establishing a portfolio that holds rock-steady high yield in its sights first, with appreciation as an afterthought. That afterthought may manifest in a much bigger way than expected.

But the stocks must still qualify on all counts. The difference is that you do not use stocks with a yield that's close to the market or only, say, twice the market, even though they may exhibit great valuation extras and strong dividend growth. You stick with the highest yielding elements that also qualify as high quality stocks with dividend growth. Today, for example, it's not that hard to create a portfolio with a 5+% dividend yield and expected dividend growth of 4% or more. As you know from earlier chapters, this portfolio has an expected return of at least 9% (current yield + growth of yield) even without anything extraordinary happening to any of the stocks. And, after about fifteen years, you'll be earning 10% on your original investment from dividends alone, with a principal value that has doubled.

But you'll probably do much better. You need to bear in mind that stocks with high yields are often out of favor and better valued than others. These are the kinds of companies to which good things—in the form of takeovers or buybacks or whatever—often happen. Indeed, in our most conservative portfolio we've held a takeover stock in each of the past four quarters, with no reason to think that the period has been especially unique.

Remember the principle: higher income generally means less risk and less total return. Lower income generally means greater growth but also greater uncertainty. Yet the world is not neat enough to follow these formulas. There will be many periods when the most conservative portfolio also shows the highest level of appreciation.

As should be clear, you can *tilt* your portfolio to suit your needs and temperament—still using only SBI-qualified stocks. You'll always want to avoid stocks that are simply the highest yielding stocks but not qualified under the SBI rules, but you can create a high-yielding portfolio simply by focusing on the high-yield SBI stocks. As you buy more "stories" and more "growth potential" your overall yield will decline, and so will the certainty and stability of your performance, though you may be in line for greater long-term total returns.

The bottom line is that your *tilt* on an SBI portfolio is an analogue to a conventional asset allocation, without the "flaw" of fixed income. Your stocks in the conventional "stock" portion are basically yield-oriented value stocks with perhaps a few beaten-down but still high-quality growth issues, and include small-cap and foreign items. (You don't have a "growth stock" allocation; there is absolutely no historical evidence that a growth stock allocation will add anything to overall portfolio returns, despite the glamour and seductive promise of this type of stock.)

Instead of fixed income you use the higher-yield breed of SBI stocks. The more income you want, or the safer you want to be, the more of this latter type you use. It's that simple.

The following paragraph appeared in the first edition of this book (1999). For obvious reasons, I've left it in:

> As I write, the overall stock market is at valuation levels among the highest ever seen. Investors believe this can last forever, just as Japanese investors believed in the 1980s. I doubt that it can— though no one ever really knows for sure. If you share that doubt you'll take the high yield road for now, possibly adding in more growth potential at some point when the market has declined and values are more reasonable. In any event, the likelihood of higher-yielding stocks outperforming lower-yielding stocks is higher when the market is more risky and vulnerable, as it is today.

That was written at the end of 1998, when the "bubble" was in full swing. Without rubbing it in too much, I can simply state that our performance has far exceeded the S&P 500 since then, capital and income has grown mightily, and we do not live with tears of regret for having bought the latest story that burst in the sky only to flame out within a few quarters. It's kind of sweet revenge, I must admit, on all those who, at the time, viewed dividends with utter disdain.

Summing Up:

1. A Single Best Investment portfolio is intended to replace a balanced or asset allocation portfolio, and shows nearly identical risk characteristics—but without the performance drag of fixed income.
2. Diversify among as many sectors and industries as you can, as long as each stock qualifies under the rules.
3. Try to include at least thirty positions. There is some academic and real world evidence that half that many may be acceptable.
4. All positions should be at equal dollar weighting.
5. You can tilt the portfolio toward higher current income depending on your needs. You may give up some capital appreciation, but in many markets you will not.

chapter 11

"THE RULES"

There are only twelve rules to follow in buying and holding a Single Best Investment stock. Still, it's important to bear in mind that rules are a tricky thing when it comes to investing, for there are always changes in the marketplace and there are always stocks whose special circumstances argue for purchase despite the fact that they may miss out on one or two points.

In 1998, as I made the final edits for the first edition of this book, the S&P 500 sold at nearly six times book value and a P/E ratio of 24, but I can remember only twenty years ago when stocks sold at less than half those measures. So investors need to be adaptable rather than rigid. Still, on a relative basis there are always higher and lower-yielding deciles of the market, there are always stocks valued more cheaply and more expensively, there are always stocks with greater and lesser relative strength. Whatever the market situation, on an absolute basis, a credit rating is a credit rating is a credit rating; and industry dominance is industry dominance in whatever time or place.

Though times do change, you should always try to stick to the rules as closely as possible. There may even be times, as when the first edition was being prepared, that you simply can't find anything to buy because the general level of prices is just too high. For all but the most sophisticated investors the rules should be seen as rules, not guidelines. If a stock doesn't fit for some reason, go find another one that does. That's one of the grand things about the markets—if the shoe doesn't fit . . . there's always another shoe. You may insist on an item that doesn't quite fit, because you "love" a stock or you use the company's products, but in that case you should remain aware that you've increased your risk. Keep in mind Warren Buffett's baseball comparison: an investor never has to swing at any one pitch—you can always wait for an item that sings in your strike zone.

Remember, we're not trying to "beat the market" here, nor are we even seeking what others might call the "best" stocks. We're trying to create a compounding machine that will be robust and durable for at least an entire investing life, one that will provide equity-market returns with some measure of reliability and predictability over time, one whose income will rise. And because its income rises the investment will also rise in market value.

It is the easy path and the sure path in the stock market, one that requires time and patience more than it requires cleverness and heroics. So don't be too clever, nor too much of a hero.

In all cases, more is better. That is, don't accept a stock if it is just on the borderline of The Rules. Look for one that's clearer, sharper, unambiguous. And never forget the basic formula:

> High quality,
> + High yield,
> + Growth of yield
> = High total returns.

The Rules

1. **The company must be financially strong.** A quick rule of thumb is that it must rate at least B+ on the Value Line stock ranking system, or BBB+ in the Standard and Poor's credit ranking system.

2. **The company must offer a relatively high current yield.** The yield should be at least 150% of the current average yield of the S&P 500, and higher is better if all other criteria are met. We prefer yields that are double the average of the broad market, or better.

3. **The yield must be expected to grow substantially in the future.** Various data services including Value Line offer expected dividend growth rates. The expected **dividend** growth rate should normally be lower than or equal to the expected **earnings** growth rate. The higher the expected dividend growth the better, but it should be at least 5% to assure growth in excess of inflation. The dividend payout ratio should be less than 50% (except utilities and REITs and limited partnerships). The past dividend growth rate can't be mindlessly extrapolated into the future, though it can provide a guide to the attitude of the company.

4. **The company should offer at least moderate consistent historic and prospective _earnings_ growth.** Earnings growth in the range of 5%–10% is _sustainable_ for a large number of companies.

5. **Management must be excellent.** A long record of success is one mark of good management. Expansion during poor economic or industry periods is a plus. Ownership of shares by management—at least one year's salary worth of shares for each top officer—is another plus. Seek management whose public statements have proven factual. New management in a "slow" company can be a major attraction—but investigate new management's past record.

6. *Give weight to valuation measures.* Price/sales ratio should be less than 1.5, and ideally less than 1.0. P/E and Book Value ratios should be less than market. Growth of cash is a big plus.

7. *Consider the "story."* Number one or number two market share in the company's industry is a positive. Restructurings are normally a positive. A price decline after an announcement to acquire another company is generally a positive, if the acquisition is not monumentally large. A tailwind in the form of substantial industry growth or favorable demographics is a positive. There should always be a "growth kicker" if possible, built on a structure of reliable cash flow. Favor companies with <u>repeating sales</u>. Consider price trends of relevant commodities.

8. *Use charts to help your buying.* There's much that's useless in technical analysis, but evaluating relative strength is useful. Prior six months of underperformance followed by notably rising relative strength is a positive. A high volume selling climax is a positive. In the short term, "look for the turn." Technicals aren't too useful for selling, but can help you sort from among candidates to buy and help in trimming your position.

9. *Picture the future.* Does the company provide a necessity of life, and execute well? Is it likely to continue to be needed in society twenty or forty years from now? Has it defeated challengers to its market in the past? Are margins improving? Is the size of its market growing? Does it dominate?

10. *Hold with equanimity.* Successful investing is about the cultivation of rational patience. Focus on the unfolding story, not quarterly earnings reports or brokerage recommendations. Keep your eyes on the far horizon of compounded growth and rising income. Avoid checking prices too often. Do everything possible to immunize

yourself against "holding anxiety." Consider taking a long trip to a faraway land.

11. *Sell when the dividend is in jeopardy, when the dividend has not been increased in the past twelve months without an excuse, or when the "story" has changed.*

12. *Diversify among many stocks that qualify as Single Best Investment stocks.* If your account is large enough, use about thirty stocks, with equal dollar amounts in each stock. To the extent that you use fewer stocks, each should be among the most conservative in the universe. The highest income stocks can still provide outstanding appreciation and total return.

Choose the Obvious Stock

All the statements below (except the last one) should continue to be true as long as you hold the stock, and you need not sell as long as they remain descriptive of your investment:

The stock has a high credit rating. The dividend is high compared to other stocks. The dividend has recently been increased. The company has reliable earnings from repeating sales and it serves a proven marketplace. Earnings are expected to rise in coming years. Margins and other financial performance measures are increasing. Management has proven itself in good times, and never been revealed to be dishonest. The company has dominance in its industry or in its geographic area. There is some kind of growth "kicker"; a new product, an acquisition, demographic trends, takeover potential—atop the base of solid cash flow. The stock fits within standard valuation measures, and may also offer some valuation "extras." Relative strength is rising in an orderly manner, ideally emerging from a prior period of relative weakness.

Let all these things be true. Let everything be in gear. If not, look elsewhere!

The hard part is sticking to the very simple parameters developed in this book. News and commentary will poison your soul. It is the devil for investors, but you can remain financially holy if you ignore all and everything, save your small shopping list of necessary ingredients.

PERFORMANCE: ACADEMIC STUDIES, HISTORIC BACKTESTS, AND REAL-TIME PERFORMANCE

Let us first say that history is history, and there is simply no rule that says that what happened in the past must happen in the future. Past performance is no guarantee of future results. This applies to actual portfolio results as well as to even the grandest and most profoundly statistical academic studies. We aren't dealing with the laws of physics in the investment world. We're dealing with economic circumstances that are always in flux, always in some kind of change, always responding to new technologies, new ideologies, always deeply the same yet always somehow importantly different. We're in a world that isn't neat enough to obey even the most elegant theories. All the study in the world can't guarantee the future will look like the past, nor that what worked in the past will work again in the future.

That's why in the very beginning of this book I tried to emphasize the need for an approach that embodies, as fully as possible, simple common sense. A sound approach should be logical, and it should be grounded in an understanding of the psychology of ordinary people. Then historical studies and actual performance can serve to confirm the sagacity of the underlying concept.

In our case, we're working with a very simple idea that happens to be loaded with common sense: if a company that offers a high dividend yield is able to continuously increase that dividend, it seems clear that the company must be making more and more money, and that a shareholding "partner" in the company will benefit from the steady growth of the business. More specifically, as the dividend rises the stock price will also rise, giving the investor a gain "on both ends," with both rising income and rising stock prices.

This very simple principle has a wealth of support in academic research, historic backtests, and in the real time performance of my firm as well as the few other managers who have implemented it. We'll look at the research as a kind of intellectual "tree," starting with work on value stocks, then high yield stocks as a subset of value stocks, then dividend growth stocks as a subset of the high yield stocks.

Value Stocks

Our Single Best Investment strategy fits in the "value" zone of the world of investment categories because the stocks tend to have lower price/book ratios than the general market (this is the standard measure for value stocks), lower price/sales, lower price/earnings, and higher yields, than stocks in general.

But often "value" stocks are seen as out-of-favor issues (that's why their valuations are low), whereas SBI stocks may fall into this shunned category, but need not. Often SBI stocks are impeccable and functioning exactly as they're supposed to, but stock investors simply don't get excited about companies with moderate and steady growth. Investors are more interested in explosive growth, or even big cyclical swings, in the often mistaken belief that they will make bigger profits just because the volatility is greater. In fact, studies have shown that there are greater profits to be made with lower-volatility portfolios than with the friskier glamour issues.

In one of a well-known series of articles in the *Journal of Finance* (6/92), professors Fama and French concluded that "firms that the market judges to have poor prospects, signaled by low stock prices and low price/book ratios, have higher expected stock returns . . . than firms with strong prospects." To understand why this should be so you must understand the slightly perverse nature of the investment world, a world in which the estimated future is always being discounted in current prices. Investors err on the side of optimism when viewing companies that are doing well, *extrapolating* profits beyond anyone's wildest dreams of avarice, imagining the potential market for a company to be larger than it is, forgetting about all that can go wrong, from technological glitches to the intense competition that arises when the scent of profitability is strong. On the other hand, when companies are doing poorly or are in areas of the market that aren't of interest to investors, investors go in the other direction and see nothing but damnation in an eternity of profitless problems for the companies they reject.

In both cases, reality proves surprising to investors. The growth stock disappoints investors' greedy imagination of how well they will do, causing investors to suddenly realize that today's price discounts more than the company can deliver, and prompting a price collapse. On the other hand, when the "value issue" performs better than expected (and little is expected, so it's not hard to surprise on the upside), its price must be "reevaluated" upward.

As Lakonishok, Shleifer, and Vishny put it, also in the *Journal of Finance* (12/94), "value strategies yield higher returns because these strategies exploit the suboptimal behavior of the typical investor and not because these strategies are fundamentally riskier. . . . A variety of investment strategies that involve buyer out-of-favor (value) stocks have outperformed glamour strategies over the April 1968 to April 1990 period. . . . Market participants appear to have consistently overestimated future growth rates of glamour stocks relative to value stocks." You might recall at this point the insight of behavioral finance—that investors are excessively overconfident in their abilities. This dovetails nicely with the excess relative performance of the stocks that investors have shown they *don't* like.

Lakonishok showed that under "laboratory" conditions (no real-time market decisions to make, no TV shows to watch or magazines or read) stocks with a low book value/market value ratio (value stocks) outperformed stocks with a high book/market by 19.8% versus 9.3%. Stocks with high cash flow per share returned 20.1%, while stocks with low cash flow per share returned 9.1%. Low P/E stocks beat high P/E stocks 19.0% to 11.4%. Considering that this set of comparisons covered the period 1963 to 1990, and considering that the prevailing attitude of academia is that the market is efficient and cannot be beaten, the numbers are impressive indeed.

As the authors put it, "A test of the extrapolation model (expectational errors made by investors) showed that while value stocks have much higher dividends and better fundamental ratios to price, investors still prefer glamour stocks due to unreasonably optimistic views on the future growth of glamour stocks. Investors' mistakes are often confirmed in the short run but then disconfirmed in the longer run." During the test period value consistently outperformed glamour in the strategies, with value stocks improving with longer time horizons (value outperformed glamour over every five-year time period).

In plain English, the tortoise beats the hare. This is not some moral value that academics would like the peasants to hold. This is the factual result of careful testing by many researchers in a large and long sample of data. It often seems as though the hot stocks are going to be the winners, and they're much more noticeable on a day-to-day or week-to-week basis. But these stocks flame out.

Indeed, according to both Lakonishok and value student David Dreman, value outperforms growth about 70% of the time, and the size of the companies involved does not seem to make much difference. Using a variety of firm sizes, returns for value stocks averaged a bit more than 7% per year greater than for growth stocks over long periods in studies by both men.

Yield Stocks

Nearly all observers agree that higher yield is an investment characteristic that moves a stock into the value category. But there has been much research on yield itself as an investment variable.

But before looking at the studies on yield, we ought to review the overall long-term importance of dividends in helping to create the long-term returns from equities that we're all so interested in achieving. In fact, many would argue that dividends (in recent years investor consciousness of dividends has become such that we might be tempted to say, "the lowly dividend") are the single most important factor in establishing investment returns.

Recall the startling numbers from Ibbotson cited in Chapter 3 regarding the impact of dividends and their reinvestment: $1 invested in stocks in 1926 grew to $76.07, while $1 with dividends reinvested grew to $1,828.33. Although dividends contributed 4.6% of a total return of 11% for the entire period, dividends were reinvested in more shares, and those shares went up, and those shares begat dividends, which begat more shares, which begat more dividends, which begat more shares, which begat sisters and brothers and cousins and uncles, each of which begat more shares, and their issue begat yet further issue; by and by you've got an epic drama with a cast of thousands!

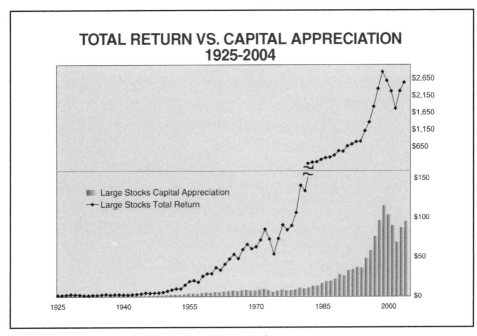

Figure A-1

In the *Journal of Portfolio Management* (Winter 1995) J. Grant concluded, in his article entitled "A Yield Effect in Common Stock Returns," that "High dividend-yielding stocks of both small and large firms were the best-performing equity investments for the thirteen-year period ending in December 1992. . . . High-yield portfolios earn abnormally high rewards in the presence of relatively low return standard deviation." Meaning, of course, that high-yield stocks were perceived by Grant as a kind of investment "free-lunch." Returns were higher despite the fact that volatility (risk) was lower. One might argue that his sample period was heavily focused on an era of declining bond rates, and that *is* a flaw—though historically the best stock returns for stocks in general have come during periods of declining bond rates.

Grant also pointed out the consistency between his findings and those of an earlier study by Fama and French. As we mentioned earlier, these two researchers concluded, in the *Journal of Financial Economics* (Vol. 22, 1988), that dividend yields can predict future stock returns and that the forecasting power of dividends increases with the length of the holding period. While yields explain less than 5% of monthly and quarterly return variances, Fama and French found that dividend differences explained fully 25% of return variances over a two- to four-year period, and that level of impact is highly significant from a statistical point of view. They tested various factors as predictors of future performance and found, for example, that the ability of earnings per share to forecast future price changes was inferior to that of dividends, because earnings are much less predictable—thus the confidence level one can have in developing expected returns is much lower.

Unlike the Grant study, Fama and French used the period 1927–1986 as their sample, a period which encompassed both rising and falling interest rate environments, and virtually everything an economy could encounter, including war, depression, out-of-control-inflation, stagflation, and healthy growth. Supporting a "dow dogs" kind of idea, the authors concluded that high yields mean that future returns will be high because stock prices are temporarily irrationally low.

O'Shaunessey's studies published in *What Works on Wall Street* (McGraw-Hill, 1996) update and confirm the earlier academic work. "It's impossible to monkey with a dividend yield," he notes, "since a company must pay, defer, or cancel it." The author found that high yield was a much more effective factor in stock price performance when what he calls "large" stocks are studied. Among large stocks, he found that the highest yielding stocks outperformed the overall universe 91% of the time over all rolling ten-year periods. He also found that when other criteria such as excellent (low) price/sales ratios and price/cashflow ratios and high liquidity are included, "large stocks with high dividend yields offer the best risk-adjusted returns available."

Interestingly, O'Shaughnessy's yield strategy showed a maximum loss that was only half the worst loss of the overall universe (a large group whose diversity "should" have mitigated risk). It outperformed large stocks in eight of eleven bear market years, had only one ten-year period in which it did not beat Large Stocks (losing out by the tiniest of fractions in performance), and *never* had a negative five-year return. Even more interesting, the yield strategy outperformed Large Stocks in nine of the thirteen years in which market gains exceeded 25%. In the very biggest bull markets, the strategy always outperformed. (Remember, gigantic bull markets invariably are accompanied by declining interest rates, and this gives an extra boost to yield-oriented stocks.) Over rolling ten-year periods, yield stocks outperformed large stocks 97% of the time. How about that for a boring and unloved group of equities!

You might note that what he calls "large stocks" is really the mid-cap universe, since it includes all stocks with a capitalization size greater than the "all stocks" database average. This works out to the top 16% of the database, or, in a nutshell, the one thousand largest stocks. This would cover the S&P 500 plus fifty (since he excluded utilities in order to prevent them from dominating a yield universe) plus the S&P Mid-Cap 400, plus another one hundred or so lurking on the small edge of the Mid-Cap Index. That's an ample universe, and I think mislabeled as large, since most institutional investors wouldn't think of stocks much below the one hundred biggest as "large." Too, there aren't very many dividend-paying issues below that size cutoff—companies have to have grown and matured enough to be able to pay dividends at all. In any event, it's certainly a big enough universe for our purposes.

One of the important points to remember when incorporating work such as Fama and French's or O'Shaunessey's into your investment thinking is that the effects of higher yield aren't really *felt* in short-term performance. As they noted, month-to-month or quarter-to-quarter performance doesn't reveal a strong impact from higher dividends. Yet, even though the longer term is made up of an accumulation of months and quarters, the effect is real and apparent when the time horizon is expanded. What explains this? The authors aren't explicit, but I believe there is a survivorship issue. Dividend-paying stocks are generally more seasoned and stronger companies; they don't swoon and die as less seasoned issues are wont to do. Also, it is inevitable that there is in fact some effect in the short term (the authors posit a 5% influence) which is magnified through compounding as the quarters pile up. It's something like inflation, which "only" grows at 4% or 2% or whatever is the current rate and isn't really felt by market participants or consumers when its happening. Only as time has gone by and the compounding effects become apparent do you realize that a car now costs twice what it did ten years ago!

Dividend Growth

This applies as well to dividend increases. In the first year, for example, you may be holding a 4% yield stock whose dividend increases 7%. Then your yield on initial investment has risen to 4.28%. It doesn't seem like a lot, it doesn't feel like a lot, until all those gains have piled up, and the growth of yield piles on top of the growth of yield until suddenly you're holding a stock yielding 10% on your initial investment. Actually, at a certain point, when your yield on initial investment has grown to over 60% (forty years) in the above example, each annual increase *doubles* your original yield— but you have to wait for that! Just as the impact of dividend yield is seen in the longer time horizons, so it is with dividend *increases*.

There hasn't been much academic work on dividend increases, but the studies that do exist point in exactly this direction, and exactly the directions we've been traveling in this book.

In the *Journal of Portfolio Management 27* (Spring 1990), John S. Brush and Anthony Spare (readers should note that both men are professionals rather than professors, and head investment firms) tested the S&P 500 stocks for the period 1968–1986, and found that the second and third deciles of dividend yield led to significant excess returns when holding periods were greater than twelve months, confirming the Fama and French as well as the Grant studies.

Brush and Spare went on to look at the issue of dividend yield *change* in what was, incredible as it may seem, the first organized inquiry into this topic (1990!). (To be fair, previous work had been done on dividend dollar-change, but that is essentially irrelevant, since only change in actual yield has any investment implications.)

The authors suggest that dividend yield combined with dividend-change may serve as indicators of investment quality for a complex of reasons. One of the most striking benefits they noted of combining dividend-yield and dividend-change is that volatility is noticeably reduced. This is of critical importance, since, as we've been emphasizing throughout this book, the real investment goal is not so much "beating the market" as it is getting equity market returns with the absolute minimum of volatility or "risk."

Unlike the yield-only results, Brush and Spare found that there was a direct performance correlation for yield-change: "the first deciles of yield-change models . . . are more successful than lower-ranked deciles in identifying positive excess return stocks . . . . In general, increasing the holding period, or increasing the change interval [time used to measure changes in yield] leads to improved first decile returns."

"This result," they noted, "is surprising in several respects. First, it is unusual to find a strategy that, even with zero transaction costs, shows increasing excess annualized returns as the holding periods get longer. Second, longer change intervals show higher excess returns than shorter intervals up to a surprising four or five years." In plain English, this latter statement means that the longer and stronger a company's dividend record, the more likely it is to provide excess returns in the future.

Next Brush and Spare *combined* current dividend *yield* with dividend *yield change*, which is the essential step in the Single Best Investment strategy. They concluded, "Holding stocks in the second, third, and fourth deciles as measured by current dividend yield, which are simultaneously in the first decile of four-year yield change [change over the past four years] for the next three years [holding period of three years], generates more excess return" than either yield or yield-change alone. When the authors combined some standard fundamental factors of the sort that we've reviewed earlier in the book, they found that "A range of combinations of fundamentals with four-year dividend change shows that long-term dividend-yield improvement used in low-turnover strategies does indeed reduce volatility, apparently faster than excess return drops."

"We conclude that dividend change, appropriately measured, does serve as an independent measure of value, providing information not found in the six [fundamental factors used in the Combo model]. The main contribution of dividend change is a marked reduction in volatility of return."

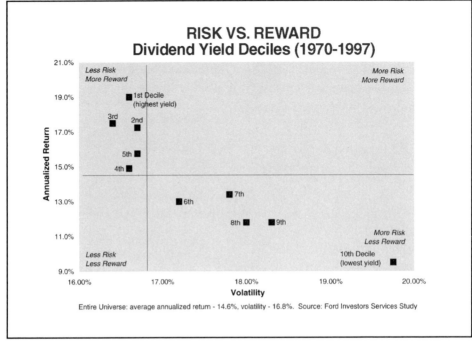

Figure A-2

Dividend Increase as a Signal

More recently, in the *Journal of Financial and Quantitative Analysis* (December 1994), authors Denis, Denis, and Sarin sought to examine the information content of dividend changes; what do dividend changes tell you about a company? They sought to find an appropriate explanation for the well-documented association between dividend change announcements and stock price changes. The authors found that changes in dividends proved to be intended or unintended **signaling** by management regarding cash flows at the company. Interestingly, though many academics had suggested companies that raise their dividends would decrease their capital expenditures (or at least not increase investments), the authors found that just the opposite is true. Companies that increase their dividends are more likely to increase their reinvestment in the business, and companies that decrease their dividends are more likely to reduce capital expenditures. The conclusion is inescapable: companies that increase their dividends are companies that are making money—enough to run a thriving business *and* enough to share with stockholders in the here and now as well.

Denis, Denis, and Sarin also note the existence of what they call dividend "clienteles," citing a fairly developed earlier literature including work by Bajaj and Vijh in 1990. Companies that raise their dividends experience stock price increases in the days surrounding a dividend announcement: it is suggested that "the price reaction to a firm's dividend change announcement is influenced by the yield preferences of the marginal investor in that firm's shares." (To an academic, a marginal investor is one who buys and sells shares, thus creating price changes—not an investor with a tattered coat!). "Investors," they note, "in high-yield firms, who place a higher value on dividends, will react positively [to an increase in dividends]." Using a sample of 6,777 dividend changes over the period 1962–1988 the authors found substantial proof for these notions: price changes for high-yield stocks are positively correlated with dividend increases. Announcements of dividend increases were met with excess returns (not explained by market movements) of 1.25%, while dividend *decrease* announcements were associated with average "excess" negative returns of -5.71%. As one might expect, the higher the dividend increase, the greater the price response. Furthermore, the authors assert, "our evidence indicates that analysts update their forecasts of future earnings on the basis of observed dividend change."

Most recently, my firm, Miller/Howard Investments, Inc., revisited the issue of high yield and dividend growth with the help of Ford Investors Services, an institutional database and research organization based in San Diego, CA. Using their database going back to 1970 we found what researchers have always found: high yield stocks outperform the market over long periods on both an absolute and a risk-adjusted basis.

We limited the universe to mid and large cap stocks in the upper third of financial strength and quality measures (we excluded utilities and REITs, since we have done extensive earlier studies on these groups). As you can see from the chart below, the ascending yield deciles bore an almost perfect correlation to higher returns.

Next, we did a regression analysis on these deciles, adding in a proprietary factor for both past and future projected dividend growth. As you can see, dividend growth acted like a turbo-charger on the highest yield sectors, without adding any volatility. In this study, yield accounts for approximately 60% weight and dividend growth 40% in the stock selection process. Portfolios were held for six months, and then rebalanced (dropouts from the top decile moved to their appropriate decile, graduates into the top decile considered an equal weight part of the decile's portfolio return).

Does all this seem like common sense to you, and perhaps not exactly worth a Ph.D.? It should, because it is, in fact, no more and no less than simple common sense. As we said in the very beginning of this book, the strategy is based on common sense. Perhaps the reason it's not a widely used strategy is that it's too common for most.

In any event, you don't have to be a professor of finance to know that if a company increases its dividend, management is saying good things about the future. It would be foolish indeed to raise the dividend if the company couldn't afford it, perhaps sufficiently foolish to open the company and management to shareholder lawsuits. There's basic human psychology at work here too: few acts are more humbling and ignominious for corporate management than to cut the dividend. Since the act of increasing the dividend a priori increases the risk of having to cut the dividend some time

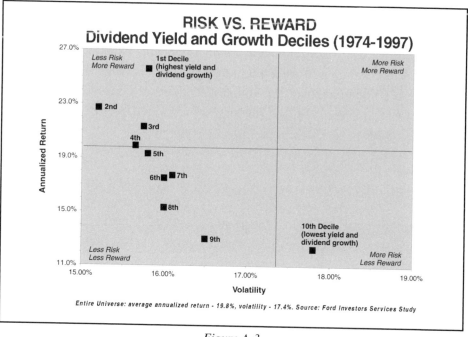

Figure A-3

in the future, management is simply not going to put through an increase unless they are absolutely certain of its affordability and viability.

Like much of social science, the academic studies confirm what we know intuitively, or have concluded logically. They can even on occasion come up with a slightly startling and seemingly counter-intuitive result, as when Denis, *et al* found that firms increasing dividends also increase capital spending. Many academics were surprised by this finding, assuming that money spent on dividends would be money diverted from reinvestment in the business. But academics are not investors, and their weakness becomes apparent when common sense is what's needed to analyze a situation. The simple fact in the real world is that success breeds success. If a company increases its dividend it's providing a marker of success—not pinching pennies elsewhere in order to please the "dividend clientele." To be sure, pleasing the latter is one of many goals, but it would never become the highest priority in a well-managed, quality company with a proven long-term record. Pleasing yield-oriented investors is a *by-product* of successfully managing a company for sustainable and consistent conservative growth, and, rather than promising everlasting growth in a world without end, sharing some of that growth in the present time.

Actual Performance

Studies are all very well, but what evidence is there in the real world that this strategy works, no matter how much common sense there seems to be in it?

In fact, there have been very few overt practitioners of this philosophy of investment. The common sense appeal of this dull and boring approach hasn't caught on with the Wall Street crowd—perhaps because it would undermine the importance of the street's much-hyped research departments. Too, starting in the late 1980s many institutional consultants began to assert that dividends weren't important—stock buy-backs were the thing, they said, and investment practitioners began to lean away from an interest in dividends.

But we have real results that are the proof of the pudding at our firm, and there are a handful of fund managers that appear to have implemented something close to what we're talking about in this book, though I can't vouch for the consistency of their discipline. What a manager does in his portfolio is not always exactly in tune with the stated strategy (if you want an eye-opening experience, check the top ten holdings of any large mutual fund that bills itself as a "value" fund. You won't believe how many high-tech stocks you'll find there!), so the other managers' performances might be a bit muddy—I have no way of knowing. There are some mutual funds that purport to follow this strategy: Fidelity Rising Dividend, T. Rowe Price Dividend Growth, Franklin Rising Dividend, and Delaware Decatur.

Our firm runs a number of strategies that are born of the Single Best Investment concept; the longest running portfolio is our "Better Than Bonds"/Utilities strategy. This one actually is the source of my insights into dividend-growth yield stocks: it worked so well with "growth" utilities that I decided to investigate further into the other sectors of the market.

What worked for utilities turned out to be a kind of eternal truth for stocks. Companies with high and persistent yields, safe dividends borne of high financial strength, a business model that provides consistent and repeating profits no matter what stage the economy is in, and moderate sustainable growth which can provide for rising income and consequent increases in the value of the stock, are the keys for investment selection.

In 1997 we started our Income-Equity portfolio, which invests in a diversified portfolio of stocks following the precepts of this book and has provided, since inception, yields higher than fixed income. The rises in income have worked out exactly as expected; an investor at inception of the strategy in 1997 would, at the end of 2004, have a *yield on original investment* of about 10%. Bear in mind, that return is from yield alone, and it will continue to rise over the years. It's significant, since most scholars of equities agree that investors should expect a total return—yield plus appreciation—of about 10% over the long term. Through wars and bubbles and the tragedy of 1991, through rising and falling interest rates and currencies, this portfolio has steadily and quietly done its job for investors.

In 1998 we also started a strategy focused on what we perceived as an inevitable consolidation in the utilities industry. This portfolio, Distribution/Merging Utilities, holds only the most conservative utilities, the distribution companies that continue to be locally regulated monopolies, which are takeover candidates. In this case, the "story of the stock" is that these are good solid companies you'd want to hold even if there's no transaction, but each would be much more highly valued in a merger. Indeed, so far about 40% of the stocks we've held have been involved in transactions, and returns have been just about the best of any equity strategy since inception (a managed account ratings agency, MMR, rated this portfolio number one for risk/reward for the five-year period ended 2004 among mid-cap managed accounts).

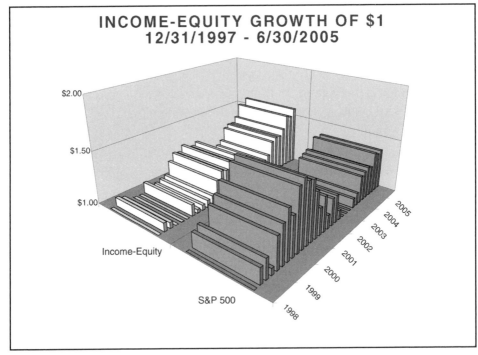

Figure A-4

THE CATEGORIES OF
SINGLE BEST INVESTMENT STOCKS

Every candidate must adhere to the "simple formula" . . . quality elements vary from industry to industry . . . utilities . . . seek a growth kicker, as always . . . REITs . . . low debt and net asset value not far below stock price, location location location . . . don't be a yield hog . . . banks . . . seek non-interest income . . . oil and gas . . . they've eaten all the fish already . . . major companies . . . pipelines a good play . . . insurance . . . sensible diversification . . . a similar "simple formula" . . . service companies . . . financial services . . . brokers . . . industrial . . . outsourcers . . . we're hooked! . . . food and "defensives" . . . cyclicals and commodity-based . . . rubies and onions in the mud . . . easy money (we ought to do a study) . . . bad odors . . . a true once in a lifetime opportunity will never be offered to you . . .

First and foremost, each SBI stock will offer the "formula" of <u>high quality</u>, <u>high current yield</u>, and <u>high growth of yield</u>.

But the features of a company which are most important in determining high quality definitely *vary from industry to industry*. Likewise, the parameters you'll use to decide if a stock "fits" the profile will vary as well. You don't ask for fabulous handling around curves when trying out a mini-van, but if you're looking at a sports car it had better stick to the road like velcro, since that's what a sports car is supposed to do. Here we'll look at some of the variable areas in different industries, lest you "screen out" categories of stocks that might be quite useful but that need to be analyzed in a modified way.

1. Utilities

Our firm has made the utility sector one of our specialties, and we've found this area to be a fruitful hunting ground, in spite of, or perhaps because of, the rejection of utilities by most institutional money managers. If you examine virtually any large mutual fund or corporate pension fund, you'll find that there is a much lower weight of utilities than there is in the S&P 500 (which is the benchmark for performance for most of these funds). Whereas the S&P 500 includes some 12% of utilities (including telephones), most professional managers hold less than 5% in the sector, and many hold none at all.

Why? While it may no longer be the case, in the past utilities never really had a "story," they never had any notable changes for managers to get excited about. Managers also were driven away by the regulated nature of the industry, perceiving the profit potential of utilities as being dampened by the regulatory ceiling. Professional investors learn from experience that most good performance comes from having a bunch of mediocre stocks and one or two great ones which drive the portfolio higher. Browsing the utilities, managers typically can't see how the field will offer the "home runs" which they need for a winning portfolio. Even worse, the folk wisdom among professional managers is that utilities won't keep up in a market rally, because their beta is much lower than the S&P 500.

So utilities have remained, for most of the century that they've existed as investor-owned companies (and most of the roughly sixty years that the universe of utilities that we know today has existed, created through the breakup of holding companies by the Public Utility Holding Company Act), the province of individual investors. Individuals have appreciated the steady flow of dividend income, and the dividend increases that have kept that income rising in excess of inflation. Individuals have been drawn to the steady performance of utilities, the fact that the stocks always manage to come back if they go down for a while, the fact that regulators have usually stepped in to bail out utilities that have run into trouble, providing a "floor" on investor returns which is in many ways more important than the "ceiling" on profits, but which is more important to individuals than professionals. Most of all, individuals have been drawn to the "common sense" of utilities, to the fact that the utility services are the necessities of life without which we cannot even survive in the civilized mode of living to which we've become accustomed. You can put off buying a new car or computer or a new dress, but you can't put off turning on the lights. You've got to have a telephone, you've got to heat and cook. You've got to drink and wash with water. Frankly, it would be easier to imagine life without any government at all in Washington D.C. than to imagine life without utilities.

And professional managers have been wrong. In fact, on a risk-adjusted basis utilities have actually performed better than the S&P 500 over the past fifty years since World War II. I know this because our firm conducted the only long-term study that exists of utilities as an asset class. We would have preferred to simply go to the library or to some Wall Street firm and read up on the long-term quantitative and qualitative performance of utilities as a group, but, incredible as it may seem, no one on Wall Street or in academe had bothered to study utilities as a long-term investment! Because we wanted to know, and because my mother taught me never to make a move without having done my homework, we undertook the study ourselves in 1990–91, accumulating data and crunching it for months on end. We were originally studying utilities to see if they were a viable alternative to fixed income.

Indeed, total returns from utilities dwarf that of bonds (we wound up calling our resultant strategy "Better Than Bonds"), but we were also surprised to find that the sector—profit ceiling and all—was totally competitive with the average of industrial stocks.

For the period of our study, 1945–1990, Dow Jones Utilities Index average annualized return was 11.75%, or 7.05% after adjusting for inflation, which averaged 4.7% during those years (this included the oil-shock inflationary late seventies and early eighties, you should recall). During the same time frame, long-term bonds returned 5.60%, or a paltry .85% after adjusting for inflation—and for much of the time bond returns were actually negative after inflation adjustment. The S&P 500 returned slightly more than the utilities at 12.25%, but the S&P 500 was almost twice as volatile as the utilities, or, as the consultants like to say nowadays, twice as risky. In other words, on a risk-adjusted basis the utilities were almost twice as attractive as the overall market. It's often said that you can't eat risk-adjusted returns (T-bills tend to have the best ratings if all you look at is risk-adjusted returns or low volatility), but in this case the returns were essentially equal to the market even before risk-adjustment.

We developed a strategy to extract the best balance of risk and reward from the utilities sector, and we've been able to exceed the long-term historic returns from utilities since 1991, even though the utilities indices have themselves been in a definite cycle of mediocre performance (failing to match historic returns).What's the strategy? It is, as you might have guessed, the Single Best Investment approach. What we've found, both in long-term research and in real-time practical application, is that high quality, high current yield, and high growth of yield is absolutely a formula that works in the utility sector. Since most utilities offer high current yield, the important features are high quality in the form of high financial strength, and growth of yield—which also implies earnings growth, a feature not always glaringly present with many utility companies. What we've found is that the *highest yielding* utilities typically offer the *worst* total returns, while the middle and lower yielders that also have some growth "kicker" are by far the best bets. Using this type of utility stock, we've been able to perform fully twice as well as the Dow Jones Utilities Index.

We look for companies with "normal" debt-equity ratios, which, in the utility area, means *about 50% debt* and 50% equity. In utilities, a moderate *payout ratio is under 70%*. We want companies to have a history of dividend increases, and a history, if possible, of exceeding their allowed rates of return. For there is only one way a utility can consistently exceed allowed rates of return, and that is by having a subsidiary or division that is unregulated and earning a higher return on equity than the utility itself. In other words, the good utilities also invariably have a "story," and the story is growth greater than mere growth of population in their territory, growth through some kind of diversification.

But beware, the utility industry is noted for its dubious record of "di-worsification," attempts to move into unrelated businesses like insurance or retail chains that have proved positively disasterous. On the other hand, companies that have diversified by leveraging their existing competencies, by moving into businesses that directly relate to their basic utility business, have often created growth environments that are powerful indeed in the regularity and consistency of their incremental earnings gains. Such gains might come from a pipeline adding fiber-optic cables to its existing rights-of-way, an electric company devising a better way to extract energy from coal, an electric company simply owning and efficiently mining substantial coal deposits, a gas distributor putting its skills to work as a "gatherer," connecting gas wells to pipelines, a telephone company buying into a high-growth country in partnership with the local carrier, etc. Steer clear, however, of diversification moves that are unrelated to the basic business. Even in related businesses, you need to watch diversification with an eagle eye. In 1998–2002 many companies went manic building new generation facilities. When everybody builds at the same time, the consequence of oversupply and nose-diving prices is inevitable, and many companies with fine long-term records were nearly ruined. So diversification can help a utility, but don't believe the hype.

In the utility sector, then, look for the following:

1. Bond credit rating at least BBB.
2. Five-year dividend growth in top two deciles of utility universe.
3. Projected five-year dividend growth and earnings in top decile of utilities.
4. Payout ratio under 70%.
5. A growth "kicker" in the form of sensible diversification or excellent growth demographics in the geographic area served.
6. Good management as demonstrated by a low cost of production and proven successful diversification ventures.

Two more utility points: What about risks? And what will change under deregulation?

One of the keys to our success in managing utility portfolios has been the avoidance of visible risk. Utilities aren't an area where you can have a gigantic winner to make up for that stinker you should have sold long ago. The group tends to move together, with just a few standouts performing much better or much worse than the average. So it's even more important than in other sectors to avoid the losers.

Will everything be different in a new era of reduced regulation for utilities? Many investors have shied away from the sector in recent years, fearing that the traditional stability of utilities would be disturbed and they would not perform well as investments. Of course we haven't found this to be the case at all, since our low-risk utility investments have actually outperformed most kinds of equity mutual funds, including many that are much riskier.

For investors, changes in the nature of utility regulation (and we are really talking about different-regulation now, not de-regulation) mean that the factors that were important for investment success in the past are now even more important, and are also more likely to generate a greater degree of relative investment success.

The key is the same as in any business where the product or service has commodity characteristics: the winner is the low-cost producer and the best marketer.

Winners under deregulation will be able to provide the highest quality service at the lowest possible price. Winners will also have the financial strength to growth their businesses, either internally or through acquisition. More than likely, winners will be able to provide more than one utility service on one bill. One day you might even see companies that provide electric, gas, telephone, cable, security—all on one bill. In any event, investors should not fear deregulation. It was only after deregulation in airlines that great companies like Southwest Airlines could appear—a winner by any measure. Only after banking deregulation could you invest in growth companies like Nationsbank (now Bank of America, after a merger), or in a smaller bank that might be taken over. Deregulation is good for investors, though the process of selecting investments may require more care and effort.

For investors who prefer their utilities in the old style, there will still be plenty of geographic monopoly companies, with rates of return regulated locally or regionally, and with "floors" on their profitability. Traditional local gas distribution companies fit the bill here, as well as water companies. As deregulation unfolds, there will also be opportunities to own shares in local electricity distributors, the "wires" companies, which should behave very much like utility shares in previous eras. Too, investors should note that in Britain, where deregulation is complete, distribution companies have proved to be among the most reliable and profitable investments.

2. Real Estate Investment Trusts (REITs)

REITs have had something of a checkered history in the past, but things have changed in this industry, and I believe every yield oriented portfolio should contain correctly selected REIT shares as long-term core holdings. REITs offer many of the same kinds of attractions as utilities, though the real estate industry is certainly more diverse, riskier, and more cyclical than the utility industry. However, REITs provide a necessity of living or doing business—just as utilities do—and REITs are likely to provide good protection against inflation, since real estate prices have historically been sensitive to inflation rates.

REITs should really be seen as a sector composed of industry groups, just as the utilities sector is composed of various service industries such as water, gas, and electric. In the REIT world, there are companies specializing in hotels, health care facilities, residential apartments, office properties, major malls, minor malls, storage facilities, industrial property, and even prisons. There are companies that employ a great deal of debt in their ownership, and others that use little or no debt. There are REITs that buy mortgages rather than real estate—these aren't part of my universe of candidates, since I focus only on equity-owning REITs which have a measure of inflation protection built into their asset base.

Most pay high dividends, since these companies are required to pass through 95% of their earnings to shareholders as dividends. The requirement is likely to decline to 90% or less in coming years, but the essential nature of the REIT structure won't change: it is more like a partnership than other stock investments, though the companies are regularly traded on the major exchanges just like other stocks, and shareholders have no greater liabilities than in other stocks. An attractive feature for individual or other taxpaying investors is that in many REITs the dividend is at least partially treated as a return of capital for tax purposes, meaning that part of the already-high yield is also tax advantaged. Further, in some REITs the dividend may be partly considered capital gain, which also receives favorable tax treatment.

What I like about the REITs I select is that they offer a high current yield, excellent growth of yield, and solid assets producing that yield. They can definitely play an integral role in creating your compounding machine. Indeed, strictly on the numbers, REITs can be seen as an appropriate replacement for utilities that have disappeared through takeovers, and for utilities that are high-cost producers and are likely to encounter problems in a new era of competition. There will always be competition in the real estate market, but REITs with good locations don't suffer from competition in any way similar to industrial or commercial companies. After all, if you possess a great location, no one else can simultaneously occupy that space!

Like the best utilities, the best REITs don't always pay the highest yields, and the best REITs will have a growth aspect that stands atop a solid base of reliable income.

Here's what to look for in a REIT:

1. The stock price should not be much higher than the net asset value of the properties the REIT owns. If it has ten dollars in real estate per share, the stock price shouldn't be much higher than ten dollars. Obviously, if the stock price is lower than the real estate owned per share it's a plus, since the company may well be a takeover candidate. A price slightly higher than real estate owned per share isn't terrible: one can make an argument that investors should be willing to pay extra for good management and good prospects as well as the liquidity REIT ownership makes possible in real estate.

2. The local economy should be in good shape. You don't have to be a financial genius to know that real estate tends to rise in value when the economy is strong, and rents remain buoyant. Of course

everyone else in the world knows which local or regional economies have been strong as well, so you may find better buys in areas that have been depressed but are beginning to recover. In such areas you'll often find the added bonus of little new construction in progress, meaning less competition for the space that's available.

3. Debt should not be more than 30% of total capital. This is a fairly conservative level for a real estate operation, but conservative is where we want to be. The last thing you want to own is property whose income can't cover its debt obligations, and the same is true of a REIT.

4. Seek a moderate multiplier of FFO. FFO is an acronym for "funds from operations," and it is the appropriate way of looking at a REIT's cash flow; it's the equivalent of earnings for an industrial company. Earnings aren't really a fair measure here, since so much income is offset by depreciation in real estate. Generally, ten or eleven times current FFO is a reasonable price for an average REIT, twelve or thirteen times for a rapidly growing REIT.

5. Yield should be middle of the road or even on the low side for the REIT universe. While very high yields are often available, there's less likely to be an element of growth present when the yield is substantially higher than average.

6. Seek growth in both FFO and yield. REITs can offer some of the highest dividend growth prospects in the entire equity universe, and can be among the most important parts for your compounding machine. Don't buy just for yield, then, but for growth of yield. In my view, REITs are typically undervalued based on potential dividend growth, though not necessarily on other factors. Conveniently, this is the factor we're most interested in.

7. Make sure there is substantial ownership of shares by management. In recent years REITs have returned to popularity, and with this return some have become candidates for fabricators of financial "products"—that is, some REITs have been created in order to satisfy investor demand for REIT shares and/or in order to exploit a market opportunity perceived by some financiers. The quick and easy security system against becoming involved in one of these comparatively two dimensional situations is to be sure that management is also a big shareholder. Management should hold at least 10% of the equity in a REIT, preferably 15% or more. When this is the case, you know that management's interests are in harmony with your own, and that management will be working as hard as possible to increase your net asset value and your cash flow. Think of yourself as a partner in a REIT (as in all other investments). Would you want the people making deals for you to have no stake in whether or not the deals worked out well? Doubtful. The more management owns, the better.

As I write, in 2005, it's almost impossible to find a REIT selling below NAV. In our Income-Equity portolio we hold only 2% in REITs, even though the yields remain strong. We believe there will be more attractive entry points in the future, and you should, too.

3. Banks

There's a "long wave" process of consolidation going on in the banking industry in the United States, and the biggest issue for investors is whether to buy acquirers or acquirees (for both offer investment advantages). A second "wave" in banking is the development of fee-based businesses by banks, and this too should be the focus of an investor interested in the industry. On occasion, one may find both trends coexisting in a single institution, but it is not common.

Generally, banks have traditionally been well represented among the ranks of companies that provide ever-higher dividends. Managements tend to be conservative—at least compared to other industries, and perhaps by virtue of the essentially paranoid nature of their basic lending business—and dividends are not carelessly raised. Most bank analysts want to talk about returns on equity, returns on assets, reserves for bad loans, etc., but I believe you'll fare just as well in the banking sector by paying attention to dividend increases and insider buying among banks that have decent quality credit ratings. In many ways it is the progress that a bank is making, the *improvement* shown, rather than its ranking on key analytic measures, which tips you off to its future as an investment.

Of course, a bank with good numbers to start with is clearly going to be more reliable than a turnaround. In the banking universe, look for a return on equity better than 12.0, a return on assets in excess of .8, and a declining level of bad debt reserves (you can be sure the market will have priced in a given level of bad debts, but it may not have priced in improvement in this measure, as investors often turn elsewhere when a bank is having troubles).

The most important factor, in this area of many investment possibilities, is *improvement*. This will be revealed in improving numbers on various measures, but, most of all, it will be revealed in rising dividends.

Many banks have done enormously well as acquirers, creating powerful regional or national franchises, but you're still likely to do better with a dividend-growth target bank than with an acquirer. After all, most takeovers occur at a market premium, and premia will increase as the number of buyable banks decreases. In the end, you're probably going to wind up owning shares in an acquirer, since consolidation is the name of the banking game in the US, so why not do it at a discount through owning a smaller, regional or even local name? When my firm first started out managing institutional accounts, we were hired by a large local bank in Nashville called Commerce Union. Commerce Union was subsequently bought by Sovran, a regional bank. Sovran subsequently merged with C&S from Atlanta, to create a larger regional. Sovran/C&S was subsequently bought by NationsBank, as, I suppose, must eventually happen to all of us. And then NationsBank became Bank of America! These transactions took place over a period of four years! This is the program, and you should assume any bank you own will get married sooner or later. Economies of scale coupled with the natural mania for power and size insure it. The good part? You get an extra incentive to hold on—the prospect of a buyout above the market price—and you find that you love your new in-law as well!

Once you've found a consistent dividend grower, look, as with other kinds of stocks, for the "story." In the case of a bank, a good story might involve growth demographics. If there's an easier way to make money than by being the banker to a rapidly growing and prosperous local economy, I don't know what it is. A story might involve a bank proving its ability to grow internally, growing all the way up to a size that makes it attractive as an acquisition candidate.

Like utilities, sensible diversification in an area that's not dependent on interest rates makes a bank much more attractive. While most banks today are actually able to manage their assets and liabilities in such as way as to make "normal" fluctuations in interest rates fairly insignificant from a profit standpoint, investors do not appear as though they will ever believe it. Rates go up, and banks go down.

But the banks that can resist rate hostility are the banks that have developed fee-based businesses. Bank of New York is the leading sponsor of foreign company ADRs, and has built a terrific business around it, a business insulated from interest rate swings. Mellon Bank is a major figure in money management, as is PNC. State Street Boston has dropped the "Boston," since it is now one of the world's largest international investment custodians, as well as a major money manager. Northern Trust is another great bank with a deep custodian business. Other banks have gotten into credit cards (not nearly as attractive as money management) and mortgages. Before long they will be doing IPOs for new companies and selling original issue bonds.

The mere fact that a bank has diversified isn't enough. Like utilities, many banks have built management staffs that are better suited to postal work than finance. So make them prove their mettle in the marketplace. The acquisition of a family of mutual funds doesn't make a bank a better bank than another bank. What makes it better is the successful integration and expansion of that business. So you need to stand aside and watch, or come to a situation after it's already been proven.

4. Oil and Gas

I have a Chinese friend who abandoned his rather successful restaurant to his sister in 1998, setting off for Vancouver where he created an export business selling ranch-raised salmon to the mainland Chinese. Salmon to the Chinese? Absolutely. As most of us know, fish is an integral part of the Chinese diet, or at least the Chinese diet as the Chinese would like it to be, something like steak in our American diet. Unfortunately (if you are Chinese) the South China Sea has basically been fished out. There is no more seafood resource to be had there anymore, and China is just beginning to develop industrially! What happens when there's a "Red Lobster" on every corner there? This is going to be the story of the twenty-first century. The sound you will hear will not be the sucking sound of jobs going to Mexico as Ross Perot once predicted, it will be the sound of the world's natural resources hurtling down the unfathomably deep abyss known as the developing world. There is barely enough oil for us in the current landscape of global development. Inventories are at historic lows and new finds are coming in at only a trickle. One of these days oil will be priced back where it was in the early eighties. It won't take a boycott to get it there, and the world economy won't be saved from inflation by a subsequent downward spiral in oil prices thereafter. This time around, when so-called experts take a wild guess and confidently predict $100 a barrel oil, they're actually going to turn out to be right! I suppose you might say that I think every investor ought to own some oil.

The kinds of stocks we can use in this area are mostly the majors, the big names you probably put in your car, since the smaller exploration and production companies are normally too risky for our type of portfolio, and they don't pay dividends. There are some twists here, however, and a "safe" way to get in on exploration and production through solid dividend paying companies that are, we might say, "half-utilities." Many of these are pipeline companies, which I include in utility portfolios in my firm because they offer the characteristics of transporters and distributors, but which may also be arguably included in the energy production area. Today, most would agree that these hybrid companies are utilities plus a diversification, but if, as, and when energy prices go skyward again—and it is certain that they will, only the timing is uncertain—these stocks will definitely perform with a speculative upside bias. In the meantime, you're paid well to wait.

The majors in general aren't really all that sensitive to crude prices, since they refine and retail products as well as produce the raw materials. When prices for oil go down, they simply make more on products, and vice versa.

But there are major international companies with large exposure to production and whose key investment characteristic is their oil and gas reserves. You should focus on these—bearing in mind that the principle of high current yield and high growth of yield still must apply (after all, what if it takes ten or twenty or thirty years for my price-gusher scenario to unfold? You still want to be a Single Best Investment holder in the meantime). Unocal, for example, has basically sold its products business and become a producer and explorer. Mobil is a play on the Hibernia field in the icy waters off Newfoundland, the biggest discovery in the Western world since Alaska.

The Spanish company Repsol and the French company Elf Aquitaine have done an excellent job building reserves globally. BP is strong in gas. Kerr-Mcgee is unloved by investors, but possesses great reserves of hydrocarbon energy. Occidental Petroleum was run almost into the ground as a one man show by Armand Hammer, investing in art collections when it should have been bidding for leases, but now the "picture" has changed at that company, and investors may see a cleaner image there as well. It is likely to turn around, slowly, like an oil tanker at sea, but the assets are there and the dividend is high, and it is the key player in newly opened Libya.

As I mentioned, many pipelines and distribution companies have become involved in energy exploration and production, and their record has been good (perhaps the more conservative nature of these companies has prompted them to bet only on the best of odds). Here we have the classic paradigm of companies with high financial strength, solid current yield, rising yield, and a growth "kicker" in a related business where they've proven their abilities. In our utility portfolios we hold Questar, Equitable, Energen, National Fuel Gas, ONEOK, among others that have added "part-time" exploration and production to their "full-time" distribution occupations. Though there's always a timeliness issue for all stocks, making one reluctant to include specific names in a book that might be read ten or twenty years from its publication date (or for generations to come, as I like to think!), these names are unlikely to disappoint as the twenty-first century develops. They'll provide high income today, rising income tomorrow, and much higher prices the day after tomorrow, when the world suffers its greatest-ever energy shortage (perhaps the last hydrocarbon crisis before photo-voltaic power becomes a commercially viable alternative).

5. Insurance

The insurance industry has its own special tricks and traps, and the gap between reported earnings versus actual revenues and cash flow can be rather greater than in many industries, due to the peculiar or unique ways in which many features of an insurance company are accounted. Fortunately, S&P and Moody's can provide some good guidance through the financial morass of insurance companies and another rating agency, A.M. Best, also specializes in the insurance industry. The complications of the insurance industry are frankly beyond the scope of this book, but that doesn't mean you won't find outstanding investments in the field.

Property/Casualty insurers might be at the bottom of your list. It's the "casualty" part that can often come up and bite you—these companies are subject to the uncertainties of catastrophic claims. To some extent that's true of all insurance companies, but your typical life insurance outfit, for example, isn't going to have a rock 'n' roll year merely because record floods happen to hit Fargo, North Dakota. Too, it seems that investors are perpetually waiting for "the cycle to turn" for PC pricing.

In my experience, the best insurance investments have been those that get farthest away from the mainstream of insurance, without becoming at the same time eccentric. Mortgage insurers have been almost uniformly good investments (could it be because they rarely have to pay off on their risks?), as have special lines companies like Frontier, and others with niches such as Hartford Steam Boiler. Reinsurers (companies that take part of the risk, usually the largest but also the "last to pay" part of the risk for regular insurers) have managed a high level of consistency, too.

Whatever the subspecialty, the key here is a long-term record of consistent moderate growth. Even if you don't really understand the precise business of a particular insurance company, you can easily understand ten consecutive years of rising earnings and dividends. There have been, and there always will be, insurance concepts that are either ill-conceived or conceived with ill will, but neither can survive the decathlon of a ten-year record of growth.

Be sure to note that requirements for low price/sales ratios don't apply to insurance stocks or banks. Return on assets measures are more appropriate for these two groups, but nothing is better than a long-term record of rising dividends combined with a current moderate payout ratio as the key to high quality.

Like banks, focus also on insurance issues with *sensible* diversification which is related to the basic business and leverages core competencies. Ownership of money management companies or mutual funds, for example, might be a logical area into which an insurance outfit could extend its expertise, as would real estate development or international expansion. The primary insurance stocks to avoid are those that do "too well." The burnouts in this industry have, in my experience, always been fabulously successful new concepts with a fly in the ointment that didn't become visible until enough ointment had been squeezed from the tube. "Hot" insurance stocks shouldn't be cause for excitement. Almost by definition, this oxymoron will not aid long-term investors.

One of the best simple valuation methods I've seen was articulated by a successful mutual fund manager who specializes in financial stocks. It looks very much like our basic high quality + yield + dividend growth formula, with an adaptive twist to accommodate the peculiarities of insurance accounting and earnings reporting: book value + dividend growth should be greater than 15% annually on a five-year rolling basis, and average return on equity should be 15% or greater as well.

6. Service Companies

It's an odd paradox: the shibboleth "that we live in a service economy" long ago became an accepted truism among economic pundits, yet if we look at the roster of top companies in the major indexes (excluding utilities) we see almost entirely companies that make *things* or sell *things*. Where are the service companies that make up this service economy?

They're out there, of course, but they're normally not the largest companies. One reason for this is that services are often provided at the local level. You wouldn't go across the country to hire a lawyer for your house closing, nor drive twelve hours for a haircut. Too, sometimes the dividing line between providing a service and selling a thing is kind of vague. Does Kinko's sell a duplicating service or expensive paper with value-added? Is the burger you buy at McDonald's a service (after all, they call it the food-service industry) or a *thing?* (Come on, this is not time for jokes!) Is your bank account a service? Your brokerage account? Is the latter a dis-service?

Financial services probably count as services, since abstraction seems to be the primary commodity when it comes to affairs relating to money. We've already discussed banks and insurance companies, leaving, in this area, niche or sub-prime lenders, and brokers of various kinds.

Recently it has come to the attention of investors that many sub-prime lenders also use sub-prime accounting methods. This is unfortunate, since the essence of the business seems to me a sound one — find ways to decrease the default rate on loans that the mainstream lenders would refuse, and charge a high interest rate to cover your losses.

This is basically the theory behind junk bonds — a theory which, after a couple of decades experience with a broad and diverse marketplace of junk, should cause the courts to lift Mike Milken's probation. Junk has been a high-return investment with less risk than the stock market. But the sub-prime lending market has a black eye, and investors need to wait now until the industry adopts and conforms to a transparent and conservative set of reporting standards. More seasoned novelty lending areas will continue to be fertile grounds for finding Single Best Investment ideas — depending, naturally, on whether the stocks are historically cheap or expensive at any given time. There's lots of potential in newer approaches that serve the underserved in the financial world but, as with nearly all investments, a long-term track record of success is worth a lot more to investors than the lucky gamble of being in at the beginning. As Peter Lynch is fond of pointing out, you could have bought Wal-Mart ten years after its first listing and still made ten times your money. Sound concepts in financial services will always have that same kind of potential to roll out nationally and grow for years and years—so seek proof and stability.

Stock brokers/investment bankers are cyclical companies. They may be reducing some of that cyclicality in recent years by increasing their fee-based money management business, but brokers are still dependent on commission flow, and the large brokers also carry large inventories of stocks and bonds. In that sense they're doubly-cyclical, since in rising markets brokers receive both more commissions and gains on their inventories, while in falling markets they get to experience a rather ugly mirror image. Even the brokers that have managed to smooth their cyclicality will be treated as cyclical by investors, just as Fannie Mae is treated as an interest rate play by investors even though interest rates have become almost irrelevant to its earnings. So buy brokers only if you are bullish on the overall market (many traders use brokers as a high-volatility proxy for the market, using them as a kind leveraged index), and don't buy brokers with the sort of "lock it up and put it away" mentality that you might otherwise use for Single Best Investment stocks.

Brokers in other areas, such as insurance brokers or real estate brokers, have often proven attractive SBI type investments. On the plus side, brokerage is a low-capital business which can be very lucrative. On the minus side, brokers are always at the mercy of the products they're selling—are the products competitive in the marketplace? Will they retain the rights to sell those products? Will they retain the fee structures they've been able to earn in the past? The larger the company, the more likely all of those questions will be answered in the affirmative. There have been some scandals in the insurance brokerage industry, but the companies are financially strong and provide needed services—they'll prosper over time.

Industrial services are more what I have in mind when I think of service companies. There are a myriad of these, ranging from giants like WMX (Waste Management) to Landaur, a small radiation-detection company which is one of my favorite Single Best Investment holdings at the moment.

Service companies can run the gamut from lawn care and janitorial services and uniform rental to temporary employment agencies and software help-desk providers. Even giant data processing and consulting firms like EDS fall into this category, as do any firms that are engaged in providing "outsourced" functionality for a company, such as doing payroll or compliance or advertising.

Services can yield great Single Best Investment opportunities primarily because these companies offer what I consider a major positive—a *recurring stream of income*. Like a utility, a recurring stream of income is what gives a company the strength and power to seek reasonable and successful ways to add incrementally to growth. Indeed, a recurring stream of income is the theoretical concept that provides the intellectual basis for the valuation of companies (a company is the current worth of the present value of its future stream of income). It's just that most companies can't really offer a recurring stream of income, they can just *hope* for one!

Once a service company gets its hooks into a client, however, it becomes a kind of unregulated utility for that client. Only the marketplace constraints of price and the cost/benefit analysis of its service inhibit profitability.

In my company, for example, we found that the level of sophistication required of our portfolio accounting software warranted a move to an outsourcing company which specializes in serving money managers with a sophisticated system to which we are attached through leased lines like an umbilical cord. We've had lots of problems getting this company to be responsive to our needs and simply to provide us with features that were promised when we signed on. On balance, we're unhappy with the provider, though their system does work and in the end has indeed saved us money. We just don't like all that we've had to go through to get there. But are we leaving? Heck no! They have all our data! We've invested a tremendous amount of time in training employees and working with this provider to get what we want. Would we start the process all over again with some unknown provider, only to discover a new set of incompetencies and lies? *No *** way!* We're hooked, for better or worse.

So service businesses can be good businesses. Companies can do well even if they don't do well (of course they'll do better if they do things right!). You'll find that many candidates aren't among the largest companies, which is fine because it probably means they're underfollowed and perhaps undervalued. Many candidates are also consolidators, which can provide their avenue for growth, assuming that they prove they can take over smaller competitors and do a good job at it. You'll find businesses in every area from data processing to garbage hauling to education, helping your efforts to diversify into various areas of the economy.

Like other SBI categories, make a sure a company has proved itself with many years of rising earnings and dividends. Don't become enamored of the latest service fad—there's a new one popping up every year. Seek recurrent income, and be wary of companies whose revenues are largely dependent on one or two large contracts. This is often the case with providers to the US government—it will behoove you to investigate the revenue sources for a company, and to determine the risk of those revenue sources drying up anytime soon.

7. Food and "Defensive" Companies

I've never understood why food and other consumer nondurable companies (soaps, razor blades, tissue paper, beer, aspirin, prescription drugs) are labeled "defensive" on Wall Street. If I'm not mistaken, this group has been the best performing category in the stock market for the past twenty years. And it is the classic area for finding Single best Investment Ideas—or it would be if most of the stocks had not become so high-priced in recent years through share appreciation!

All the ingredients we look for are here: recurring revenue, value in brand names and distribution in addition to the bricks and mortar of the company, a large and inelastic end-user marketplace, ample opportunities for growth through acquisition, brand extension, international expansion, etc., "proof of the pudding" through a long history of consistent earnings and dividend growth through all kinds of economies. (Actually, these stocks are called "defensive" because they don't lose money during recessions, or at least not as badly as more industrial types. But they also make money when the economy is fine. Wouldn't "defensive/offensive" be more appropriate?) In the end, our simple goal is to find companies with high probabilities of earning more and paying more in dividends in the years ahead than they do today. Food, drink, drug, and hygiene companies have been doing this for decades, since the beginning of our economy, really, and are as likely as any to keep doing it for decades more. As long as people are going to reach for a Hershey Bar, or have a can of soup for lunch, or brush their teeth, or wipe their bottoms, or take an antibiotic, these companies will be making money. And, to the extent they can establish a brand or intellectual property rights (such as a patent), they will have real or pseudo-monopolies on their markets.

These kinds of stocks are great buys when the market goes down, or when there's a temporary problem with one of the companies and investors become scared, ready to hand over shares at a discount (remember how Johnson and Johnson declined sharply during the Tylenol scare some years ago. You can't even see that dip on a long-term price chart today, but back then you were offered a temporary 30% discount on the shares). These stocks are like the Colorado River and the Rockies and The Great Plains and the Panhandle—fixtures of the American economic geography that are never going to go away, and which should always be bought when "on sale."

8. Cyclicals, Commodity-Based, and Others

In the passages above we've looked at the categories of stocks where you're most likely to find Single Best Investment candidates for your portfolio; utilities, REITs, banks, insurance, financial service, industrial and commercial service, the classic consumer nondurable areas of food, drink, drugs, and hygiene.

What about the rest of the economy? What about the things that go clank, and the things that plug in, the things that ship by truck trailer, the cars and planes and boats and trains that we ride in, the nuts and bolts that hold them together, the pumps that bring water to the faucet, the fans that move the air? And what about the metals they're made of, and the plastics, and the chemicals that clean them, and the buckets the chemicals come in, and the forklift trucks that move them? What about the whole edifice and infrastructure of industrial American, the smokestacks and warehouses and rail yards and endless parking lots filled with armies of workers who support the assembly lines to the ends of their days?

Here we will find the interesting odd situation that may well inspire us to think of T.S. Eliot's line "garlic and sapphires in the mud." But discoveries won't be typical in this realm because of the cyclicality of the businesses. You may know the name International Paper, but it's in a business that traditionally yo-yo's in pricing and in demand patterns, and such an environment, while not devoid of investment possibilities, is not generally going to yield up the kinds of reliable vehicles we seek. When you buy a paper company, for example, you've got to know all of the trends in paper pricing (and in wood products generally). And not just paper pricing: there's newsprint, white paper, glossy paper, specialty paper, pulp, on and on. Not only do you have to know the pricing trends, you have to know how long they will persist and what the odds are of a reversal of fortune.

In effect, when dealing with a cyclical stock, you're back to playing the market! Just the thing we're trying to avoid! Attempting to outguess all these timing considerations creates an environment ripe with potential for error. And it's not even worth the effort, for cyclical companies over the long term do not have a better investment record than moderate steady growth stocks. So why bother with them? To catch the occasional tailwind in a commodity? I don't think that's our game.

That said, however, there are situations in this area that may fulfill our guidelines. Many industrial companies actually aren't especially cyclical. We own a company called Federal Signal, for example, which specializes in making fire engines. That's not a business that depends on the cycle of recessions or car buyers or whatever. It just depends on them making a better fire engine and making a profit at it. When times are a bit slow this company gets unloved and sells for a high yield. When investors bail out, value players spot a gem and begin to buy it. The stock gets to be a bit cyclical, but the *basic underlying business* is not. So each low in price gets higher as the years go by. There are many stocks like this, makers of ball bearings (Timken) or fuel storage tanks and railcars (Trinity) or distribution and processing of steel (Worthington) that are fine, conservatively managed companies which do have regular and recurring revenues and should definitely be bought on dips when they are out of favor. The ride may not be as smooth as with the more classic recurring revenue companies, but there's no law saying you can't sell at a high point, and many of these stocks will also prove to be takeover candidates as the years go by.

What about commodity plays like Phelps Dodge in copper or Alcoa in Aluminum? These are excellent for some *other* investor with a different philosophy. Commodity prices swing up and down, dragging the related stocks with them, making earnings and dividends unpredictable. Investors don't like uncertainty, and since we're investors, we don't like companies that are clearly and unequivocally cyclical.

9. Easy Money

Here's a nifty idea that's especially suited to our types of stocks—the types that always come back and rise higher after they've been down. Unfortunately, this is anecdotal, in the sense that I haven't done a good statistical study on the situation and I don't believe there is anything in the academic literature either. But it's an excellent gambit that I've acquired through experience and observation, and I think if you watch these occurrences for a while you'll soon agree. I'm not giving away the store, I hope, since the forces that create this opportunity are unlikely, by definition, to ever lose their impact.

Because greed is such a powerful psychological force in the marketplace, investors are constantly looking for takeover candidates, for stocks offering the possibility of an instant win. I can't claim to be immune to this quest and, indeed, because Single Best Investment stocks represent such good value, they often do become the object of offers from acquirers.

Likewise, investors often shy away from acquiring types because the price of the acquirer often declines when it makes an offer for another company. If the company is going to get bigger through its acquisition, why does the price decline?

There are basically two reasons. First, Wall Street may not like the deal, either because analysts don't think the merger is a good "fit" or because the terms of the deal mean that it will actually diminish the acquiring company's earnings in the first year or two after the merger.

Second, lurking in the caverns of the financial district are roaming packs of arbitrageurs. Since the price of the target company rarely rises to the offering price right away (the deal will take time, which involves an opportunity cost relative to another use of the investors money, and, in addition, there is always a risk that the deal will fall apart—causing the target company's price to drop), arbitrageurs sell the acquiring company short and buy the target. In this way they earn the "spread" between the current price of the target and the eventual deal price, while also hedging against an increase in the price paid for the target stock.

This arbitrage pressure causes the price of the acquiring company's stock to drop. If investors don't like the deal, the pressure on the acquiring company's stock is further magnified.

So what do we have? Company A makes an offer to buy company B. The stock of company B's stock rises, but not all the way to the offer price. The price of company A's stock drops because arbitrageurs hoping to earn the difference between today's price and the deal price sell A short while buying B. If the deal is at all dilutive, A's price drops even further, adjusting to an impending downward revision of A's earnings for the next year or so.

But why would A make an offer to buy B if the only result is going to be a drop in A's stock? Of course no company would engage in such suicide. A would only buy another company because A's management believes it will make A better. And, indeed, the list of companies who have grown and prospered through acquisitions is literally endless. Great companies are always becoming greater through acquiring complimentary companies or even competitors. (As anyone knows, the best business is an unregulated monopoly.)

Though acquisition is a key method for companies to grow, it is the mechanics of the marketplace that causes their stocks to fall when they offer for another. Arbitrage activity drives the stock down, and the obsessive focus of investors on every penny of earnings drives the stock down. The instant decline of the acquirer isn't really a "vote" on the perspicacity of the acquisition, it is merely the secular turning of wheels on the stock exchange.

But the opportunity here lies in the fact that the pressure on the acquiring company is not only artificial, it is also temporary. As the deal nears fruition the spread between current price for the target company and the ultimate transaction price narrows and narrows, until there is finally no arbitrage profit in it at all. At that point, or, at worst, on the day the deal is consummated, the arbitrage positions are closed, and all who were short the acquirer have now become—guess what?—buyers! As the acquiring company is bought to close out these positions and the arbitrage pressure relents the stock price rises back to where it "should" have been in the first place. Pressure on the acquiring company may still be present due to fears of dilution, but those views too may have changed in the interim.

In any event, investors in high quality stocks that have proven themselves through various economic conditions and have proven themselves to be adept at digesting and enhancing acquisitions need not worry. Time will recover any near-term earnings dilution, and investors will be left with a larger, better, more profitable company.

While this little angle may not have enough substance to form the basis of an overall investment strategy, it is a nifty contrarian device for generating essentially unearned profits in the market. More important, when a solid Single Best Investment company of the sort that you want to hold for a lifetime suddenly sells off because it's doing the kind of thing that's made it great in the first place, step up and be a buyer. You're getting premium merchandise on sale. And this is really the only unambiguous sale counter I know of in the market. There are other times when you can buy a fine stock on a "dip," but those times are usually accompanied by the anxiety of a bad earnings report, a management crisis, or a selloff in the market generally.

10. Bad Odors

We've discussed some of the kinds of information that should make a stock repellent, but these factors can never be stressed too strongly. It is the losers that really hurt you in investing—they hurt more than the winners help. Who hasn't heard of the basic bit of investment arithmetic, that the impact of a negative return is greater than the impact of a positive return? If you lose 50% on an investment you need a 100% return to break even. If you make 100% on an investment, a 50% loss will put you back to zero. If you gain 50% and then lose 50%, you're down by 25%. Ugly numbers.

Here are some features that should cross a stock off your candidate list or should provoke serious thought about selling if you hold it:

- Quarrels with the company auditor, or firing the auditor during a time of controversy over earnings.
- Federal investigations.
- Questions by anyone in an official capacity regarding the timing of recording revenues and expenses.
- Successful and legal sales by insiders just prior to announcements of bad news or earnings shortfalls (it's never too late to flee a sinking ship).
- Great sales of a new product at the wholesale level, but with questionable sell-through at retail.
- Claims of mineral or energy resources unverified by objective third parties.
- Breech of loan covenants (this should never happen in your portfolio, since we screen out companies with high debt loads).
- Changes in governmental rules or programs from which the company has previously benefited.
- Profits that are highly correlated with changes in currency values.
- Dividend yields that are just too high, compared to other companies in the industry and the company's earnings.

- Earnings that rise when revenues are not (assuming that the company has not sold or closed divisions).

You're not likely to encounter these "smells" in a true Single Best Investment stock, since high quality companies can't ordinarily compile long-term records of earnings, revenue, and dividend growth if they tread near these no-nos, but I state them because I've never known an investor who could easily resist a story that seemed too good to be true, even though in our saner moments we all know that if it "seems" it probably "is." In a way, the real message is this: be content with what's good and solid and works. If an investment is honestly and truly a once in a lifetime fabulous opportunity, you can pretty much count on the fact that it won't be available to you. Nothing personal, but why would any sophisticated professional let that really astounding item fall into your hands?

INFORMATION RESOURCES

As I've noted, the world is now inundated with investment information. To attempt to provide a full and complete listing of all the sources to which an investor can turn today would require a book in itself. The following brief summary will lead you to easy, inexpensive, and readily available sources of the kinds of information you'll need to put the principles of The Single Best Investment to work—plus a few items that I believe will be of general interest to all investors.

1. Value Line. This compendium of data is available in most libraries, and you can subscribe to their extensive weekly updates. While the same data is available in many other places, Value Line is unique in its display of data covering many years. You can see the trend of dividend increases over time at a glance, for example, as well as the trends of sales, earnings, cash flow, cash available, and virtually every other valuation measure you can think of—all laid out in a quick reference spreadsheet style. I don't pay a great deal of attention to the advisory text, but you will find in the text information about changes, restructurings, or upcoming changes in corporate prospects. Located in the index section you'll also find regular screens indicating the highest yielding stocks as well as stocks with projected highest future yields. Value Line also puts out a screening program which is useful as a preliminary step in creating a universe of investment candidates. The Value Line Investment Survey, 220 East 42nd Street, New York City, New York, 10017.

2. Standard and Poor's. The "little gray book" is available from most brokers and also provides a wealth of data in spreadsheet format. There are few screens or advice here, but it's a nice portable data summary which you can take on the plane or keep in the bathroom. The company also publishes a variety of market data and advisory services. They have a somewhat stuffy reputation, but I find them accurate and sensible. Standard and Poor's, 25 Broadway, New York City, NY, 10004

3. Morningstar. Morningstar also has a stock service which is similar to Value Line, but which I haven't really used. You'll also find "quicktakes," which are useful data snapshots, on their website. Morningstar, 225 West Wacker Drive, Chicago, IL 60606.

4. Internet Sites. The internet is a great way to use up time, a kind of interactive form of television. It is loaded with sites for quotes, charts, data, and comment, as well as some sites where you can perform screening for candidates at little or no charge. There are also numerous sites which will keep you abreast of market news, and which also include articles on various investment subjects, if that's your idea of a good time. The SEC has done a great service to investors by requiring companies to release relevant investment information in a timely manner on public services such as BizWire and PRWire, and these releases are reproduced in many areas on the internet. One word of warning regarding internet database information: double-check your data before actually using it to make an investment. You can always call a company's shareholder or investor relations office to verify the figures on which you're basing your conclusions. In my experience, essentially all the databases available on the internet are "dirty" and need verification.

a. Microsoft Investor (moneycentral.msn.com/investor/home.asp). This site is a great bargain, in which you can find screening tools, company summaries and data, charts, news, market summaries, quotes, you name it.

b. Briefing.com (www.briefing.com). This site will help you keep up on the news, which is of ancillary importance, but there are also nice features and tools, such as the ability to read at a glance all the important news stories about a company over the past two years, calendars for economic and earnings reports, etc.

c. Multexnet (www.multexnet.com). This one costs quite a bit. It is a compendium of research reports from brokerage houses. I never trust the conclusions of brokers—there are too many conflicts of interest and too few of the analysts have any sense of valuation—but Wall Street analysts are indisputably good at collecting all the relevant information and painting a picture of the company's "story."

d. Morningstar (www.morningstar.com). Morningstar has mutual fund screening where you can find out how all the different categories of mutual fund have been doing right up to the day on which you're screening. There is also a nice "quicktake" section which will give you an instant overview of a company, including financials and price action.

e. The Wall Street Journal (www.wsj.com). *The Wall Street Journal* is available online in a somewhat abbreviated version, but one which includes all the important stories, the "meat." There is also a "briefing book" section which provides a great deal of data about individual stocks, from charts to news to financials. You can also link to Barron's from the site.

f. Bloomberg (www.bloomberg.com). Bloomberg online provides concise updated news stories, summaries of stocks moving in the markets, stocks likely to move the markets in upcoming sessions, and a variety of columns.

g. Nearly every significant magazine, newspaper, broadcaster, and stockbroker has a site—you can save money and trees by accessing your favorite magazines and papers on the internet. Some have archival search features, so you can look for a history of articles on the stocks you're interested in. Sites with which I'm familiar and which may be of interest include (all are "www" sites) **forbes.com, worth.com, money.com, smartmoney.com, nytimes.com, cnbc.com, schwab.com, dlj.com, cnn.com, etrade.com**—the list goes on and on. Search Yahoo or Lycos for "investment" "sites only" and you'll be inundated. Yahoo also has its own finance site that is a stop of interest. Just one observation about internet information: there's too much of it and it's updated too frequently. It acts like coffee on your investor's nerves, and this is often not such a good thing.

5. Newsletters. I don't think much of newsletters, and it appears that many newsletter writers are not really qualified to hold a regular job, much less give investment advice. But I do peruse the offerings from time to time, in hopes of finding intelligent and hardworking independents who might make my job a little easier. I don't profess a thorough knowledge of the entire arena here, but have stumbled upon a few where I am at least willing to go beyond a trial subscription—these will usually have at least one or two good ideas worthy of further research, and sometimes more than that.

a. Utility Forecaster. Roger Conrad, ed., KCI Communications, Inc., 1750 Old Meadow Road, McLean, VA 22102.

b. Profitable Investing. Richard Band, ed., Phillips Publishing, Inc., 7811 Montrose Road, P.O. Box 60042, Potomac, MD 20859.

c. Oil & Energy Investment Report. Bob Czeschin, ed., 12254 Nicollet Avenue South, Burnsville, MN 55337.

d. Intelligence Report. Richard Young, ed., Phillips Publishing, Inc., 7811 Montrose Road, P.O. Box 60042, Potomac, MD 20859.

e. Income Digest. P.O. Box 21130, Ft. Lauderdale, FL 33335-1130.

Again, I'm sure there are many more worthy newsletters I've missed. These are probably worth their subscription prices, in my limited experience. One more, **Standard & Poor's Advisor**, is available free from many brokers and mutual fund families, including Fidelity.

6. Charts. In recent years charting has become a kind of mania among people interested in the market and there are tons of programs to do charting yourself as well as tons of sources on the internet that offer charts. All this action is not because charts are such a wonderful tool. Rather, it is very easy to program a computer to create charts, and then you have something interesting to look at on your screen, as well as a kind of game where the options for making changes are virtually unlimited, meaning you can spend an unlimited amount of time viewing data which is of very little help to you over the long term.

Some easy ways to get updated charts are websites: **www.cbsmarketwatch.com, www.bigcharts.com,** and **www.investors.com** (Investor's Business Daily). I like the charts from Securities Research Company, **www.srcstockcharts.com,** many of which were used in this book.

Some Books of Interest for SBI Investors:

What Works on Wall Street, James O'Shaughnessy, McGraw-Hill, 1997

Stocks for the Long Run, Jeremy J. Siegel, Irwin Professional Publishing, 1994

Contrarian Investment Strategies: The Next Generation: Beat the Market by Going Against the Crowd, David Dreman, Simon & Schuster, 1998

The Dividend-Rich Investor, Joseph Tigue and Joseph Lisanti, McGraw-Hill, 1997

The New Money Masters, John Train, HarperCollins, 1989

Classics: An Investor's Anthology, Ellis and Vertin, Dow Jones Irwin, 1989

The New Stock Market, A Complete Guide to the Latest Research, Analysis, and Performance, Fabozzi, Fogler, Russell, and Harrington, Probus Publishing, 1990

Stocks, Bonds, Bills, and Inflation Yearbook, Ibbotson Associates, annual

The Dividend Investor, Harvey C. Knowles and Damon H. Petty, Probus Publishing, 1992

Dividends Don't Lie, Geraldine Weiss, Longman Financial Services Publishing, 1988

The Dividend Connection: How Dividends Create Value in the Stock Market, Geraldine Weiss, Dearborn Trade, 1995

The Intelligent Investor 4th Rev., Benjamin Graham, HarperCollins, 1996

Extraordinary Popular Delusions and the Madness of Crowds, Charles McKay, Crown Publishers, 1995

Organizations:

You can get information on listed companies and exchange-traded funds (including company phone numbers) from:

The New York Stock Exchange—212-656-3218
The American Stock Exchange—212-306-1490

And on "NASDAQ" companies from:

National Association of Securities Dealers—301-590-6578
(Also see the websites for these organizations)

And on all publicly traded companies from:

Securities and Exchange Commission EDGAR database of company filings at **http://www.sec.gov**

A FINAL WORD:
THE HUMAN FACE OF DIVIDENDS

We were recently perusing a paper by Adam S. Koch and Amy X. Sun of Carnegie Mellon University in which they tested 6,395 dividend change announcements made by 1,682 publicly traded companies between 1983 and 1999 (compared to over 37,000 "no change" cases), in quest of several hypotheses regarding the meaning of dividend changes with respect to past and future earnings changes.

While most observers consider dividend changes to be an information cue about the future prospects of a company, Koch and Sun take a different tack, one which is quite timely in this age of a general culinary approach to corporate bookkeeping (most recently it has turned out that Fannie Mae was lying all along). Rather than focus on dividend increases as a message from management about the future (Healy and Palepu, 1988), they have determined that dividend changes are a kind of certification of previously reported earnings changes—just as valuable for investors, though the focus is more on the past than the future. Dividends become a tool for investors to determine the persistence of earnings changes, which is, said differently, all about the credibility of past reporting.

To quote their abstract, "We examine whether the market interprets changes in dividends as a signal about the persistence of past earnings changes. Prior to observing this signal, investors may believe that past earnings changes are not necessarily indicative of future earnings levels. . . . Results confirm the hypothesis that changes in dividends cause investors to revise their expectations about the persistence of past earnings changes. This effect varies predictably with the magnitude of the dividend change and the sign of the past earnings change."

In other words, the authors are suggesting, and we agree, that investors are in a perpetual state of anxiety about the reliability of the information they've already received from management, and that when a dividend change confirms earlier reports investors are willing to reduce the necessary skepticism that is always a conscious or unconscious factor in their valuation equation.

To bring this down to earth, which we find necessary after parsing the authors' formulas (which often run a full two lines including much decoration with Greek letters in a simulacrum of algebra), if you're getting cash that means the company actually made the cash. Whether you as an investor look at it as a certification of the past or a message about the future isn't that important. What matters is that you've been given some proof of the "statements," and though there have been a few scam dividends in the past, handing out cash isn't usually the way crooked or self-serving managers operate. The end result is that an investor can mark up the valuation of the company that increases its dividend because in a world characterized by the everlasting tension between promise and certainty, at a minimum the certainty side of the equation has been strengthened.

In what we might call the Dividend Dark Ages covering 1990–2003, the armies of MBAs occupying the intermediary slots in the investment food chain insisted that dividends were foolish, that book entries are the same as money, and we should trust our corporate managers to wisely invest surplus earnings in ever greater growth, or, at worst, to buy back stock and kite the value of our holdings as well as their options.

As we know, this philosophy among investors has amounted to granting managers of publicly held corporations a license to kill, or at a minimum the license to manipulate share prices through devious accounting—which is perfectly understandable since the bulk of their compensation is in shares.

Anti-dividend philosophies have been concocted by academically trained functionaries who forget that investing isn't about the numbers that are so easily melted in spreadsheets or "massaged" in investment strategy modeling software. Investing is about a human relationship between someone with capital and someone who needs that capital to make or sustain a business.

Let's say your acquaintance wants to start a hip fashion boutique. You think he (or she) understands the business and can manage it, so you invest some money. A little soft on your manager and the pro-forma profits outlined in the business plan, you take stock in the venture, as a minority holder. A location is found, a lease is signed, the shelves are stocked and the sign goes up; before you know it there's a grand opening with colored flags and a full-page ad in the local paper. Ka-ching, Ka-ching, little skirts and hoop earrings are moving out the door to the seemingly constantly filled parking lot.

By and by it seems that the business is quite profitable, and you think you should share in the profits. But your manager says whoa, he's got a line on a great location for a second store. Business has been so good that he can open it from funds internally generated, no need for additional capital, so now you're going to own a piece of two stores, not just one, for no additional investment! The prospect of growth for your investment quiets you down, and any misgivings you might have had about the cost of your manager's new home and new Porsche seem to fade as you count on your fingers how much two stores might be worth.

Of course this calculation is significantly impacted by the future promise of value, rather than any present return. Of course boutiques do have a market value, roughly speaking, and you can determine what one store and two stores that are profitable might be worth to a buyer, but until there's a buyer you have only the promise. There is only theoretical value without a transaction.

You think maybe you'd like to have a nice new car, too, so you raise the issue of distributing profits once again. But once again your manager has a plan for expansion—this time for a mega-boutique in the new mall that's going up. Rents are premium there, but the retail traffic should be incredible. And so you wait, once again, while the investment you made has babies and more babies, and its babies have babies.

One can see where this is going, and we needn't reveal the ending by announcing the ultimate fate of the business. The simple fact is that an investor is always caught in the dialectic between the certainty of a cash return now and the promise of a greater return later. Why is it so difficult for investors to insist on some level of balance between the two?

Why do investors persist in accepting the projections of managers about the future without taking in some real return from the accomplishments of the past?

This is the human face of dividends, the true actuality of dividends: you invest money in a business and the business pays you back some of its profits in real time, while retaining enough for sustainable and reliable future growth. You receive confirmation of present success, you receive a return on your investment which is minimally a hedge against future failure of the business, you receive a share of profit which goes to the investor and not the manager (this is only fair), and you retain a position in the business which can bring you more of the same indefinitely.

What strange twist of the psyche would have it any other way?

FEEDBACK

I'm always interested in hearing from investors, although life is short and I may not have time to respond to every comment or inquiry. The most likely way to stir up a reply would be to e-mail me:

lowell@mhinvest.com

To receive standard firm information, e-mail:

marilyn@mhinvest.com

or visit our website, **www.mhinvest.com**

If you wish to write, the address is:

Miller/Howard Investments, Inc.
324 Upper Byrdcliffe Rd.
P.O. Box 549
Woodstock, N.Y. 12498
or fax at 845-679-5862

Please don't call: we're a boutique firm and the extra burden of responding to curious phone calls is very disruptive. We have been in business since 1984, and as of this writing we have over $1 billion under management.

Our firm is registered with the Security and Exchange Commission and offers private account management for investors with at least $250,000, based on the principles in this book, with greater or lesser emphasis on income depending on the investor's needs.

We also offer an absolute return strategy, which is something like having your own private hedge fund, for qualified investors.

We work with numerous brokers and financial consultants across the country. Your broker or consultant may be able to make the connection with us, or we can suggest someone in your geographic area if you don't currently have help and would like the benefits of broad financial planning and custody at a major firm.

INDEX

ABOUT THE AUTHOR

Lowell Miller has been an investment professional for over thirty years, and has systematically investigated nearly every approach to investing during his career. After graduating from Sarah Lawrence College and New York University School of Law, Miller began managing an options hedge fund while still in his twenties.

He is the author of two previous books on investing (the first of which, *The Momentum-Gap Method,* G.P, Putnam's, 1978, was named "Investment Book of the Year" by the Hirsch organization), and has written on investment-related subjects for *The New York Times Magazine*. In 1984 he co-founded Miller/Howard Investments, Inc., which today manages over $1 billion based on the principles outlined in this book. At Miller/Howard, in addition to his role as Chief Investment Officer, he has also conducted and supervised many novel and original studies of stock price and asset class behavior.

While it might truly be the subject of yet another book, Miller/Howard portfolios are also socially screened to exclude companies involved in alcohol, tobacco, firearms, environmental damage, poor workplace relations, etc. It is the view of the firm that there are many good options for investing which include socially responsible companies; most often responsible corporate behavior leads to more profitable companies with less regulatory and legal risk, and better workforce morale.

Lowell Miller has been a featured guest on Louis Rukeyser's *Wall $treet Week,* and his investment insights frequently appear in such media as *The New York Times, The Wall Street Journal, Barron's, Investor's Business Daily, Forbes,* and *Bloomberg.* In his spare time he is a writer, sculptor, and 5th degree black belt in Aikido, a Japanese martial art of self-defense.

In *The Single Best Investment* he makes available the fruits of a career in both investment management and investment research to investors at every level of sophistication. He reveals the secrets of professional investing, through a clear and concise plan that any investor can emulate.